BILL GATES,
PAY YOUR FAIR SHARE
OF TAXES...LIKE WE DO!

BILL GATES,
PAY YOUR FAIR SHARE
OF TAXES...LIKE WE DO!

Brigitte Alepin

Translated by Bob Chodos, Eric Hamovitch
and Susan Joanis

James Lorimer & Company Ltd., Publishers
Toronto

James Lorimer & Company Ltd., Publishers acknowledges the support of the Ontario Arts Council. We acknowledge the financial support of the Government of Canada through the Canada Book Fund for our publishing activities. We acknowledge the financial support of the Government of Canada, through the National Translation Program for Book Publishing, for our translation activities. We acknowledge the support of the Canada Council for the Arts which last year invested $24.3 million in writing and publishing throughout Canada. We acknowledge the Government of Ontario through the Ontario Media Development Corporation's Ontario Book Initiative.

Cover photo: iStock

Library and Archives Canada Cataloguing in Publication

Alepin, Brigitte
    Bill Gates, pay your fair share of taxes...like we do! / Brigitte Alepin; translated by Bob Chodos, Eric Hamovitch and Susan Joanis.

Includes index.
Translation of: La crise fiscale qui vient.
Issued also in electronic formats.
ISBN 978-1-4594-0035-1

    1. Internal revenue. 2. Fiscal policy. 3. Tax planning.
4. Tax administration and procedure. I. Chodos, Robert, 1947- II. Hamovitch, Eric III. Joanis, Susan. IV. Title.

HJ2318.3.A4313 2012   336.2   C2011-908388-4

James Lorimer & Company Ltd., Publishers
317 Adelaide Street West, Suite 1002
Toronto, ON, Canada
M5V 1P9
www.lorimer.ca

Printed and bound in Canada.

CONTENTS

ACKNOWLEDGEMENTS

I take full responsibility for the contents of this book. However, I could not have completed it on my own, and teamwork played a large part in bringing it to fruition. Therefore, I would like to express my deep appreciation to the bright, effective and courageous young researchers who worked on this project: Julie Larocque, Chanel Alepin and Maxime Alepin. Cherished colleagues, thank you.

Même si j'assume la responsabilité complète de sa teneur, ce livre est le résultat d'un travail d'équipe que je n'aurais pu mener à bien toute seule.

Je tiens donc à remercier chaleureusement Julie Larocque, Chanel Alepin et Maxime Alepin. De jeunes chercheurs intelligents, efficaces et courageux.

Merci chers collègues.

PREFACE

Bill Gates, pay your fair share of taxes...like we do.

When I showed this title to my brother, he said (with a smile), "How dare you speak to Bill Gates that way. He's like a god!"

This book may change the way you see your superheroes. I'm not putting any of them on trial. They're not the ones who are primarily responsible. It's the system, and that's what this book is about.

INTRODUCTION

According to *Forbes* magazine's calculation, Bill Gates was worth $59 billion in November 2011.[1] The magazine did not present the details of its calculation,[2] but it is quite possible that a significant portion of this amount is attributable to the gap between what Gates and the companies he runs (or ran) should be paying in taxes and what they actually pay.[3] You might be surprised at just how large that gap is. Warren Buffett pays taxes at a rate of 17 per cent.[4] In some American states, the statutory rate (federal, state and local) for someone at his income level could reach 45 per cent.[5] There is no doubt that the wealth corresponding to these unpaid taxes belongs legally to Mr. Buffett, but at a time of crisis, we can't help being struck by the size of the gap.

Mark Zuckerberg has not publicly revealed his effective tax rate. However, he moved part of Facebook's operation to Ireland in 2008.[6] If we make the reasonable assumption that the value of Facebook has grown from $20 billion in 2008[7] to $100 billion by the end of 2011,[8] then the decision to move part of Facebook's operation to Ireland could represent a savings of billions of dollars in taxes.

Warren Buffett's low tax rate may well be due to the fact that he has transferred some of his wealth to the Bill and Melinda Gates Foundation, and in that case it could be justified by the social contribution he is making. If this were so, then public accounts could logically be said to balance if the tax benefit offered to Mr. Buffett was equal to the benefit society derives from his contribution.

However, since the Gates Foundation rarely spends more than the return on its capital, this is not the case.[9] Many private foundations have adopted this modus operandi. By conserving their capital, private foundations are able to remain in existence in perpetuity. In a time of crisis, we should question if this is something our societies can afford to finance.

The situations of Bill Gates and Mark Zuckerberg are typical, and they provide a good illustration of just how illogical our system is. Around the same time that several billion dollars in taxes had been saved by including Ireland in the corporate structure of Facebook, Mark Zuckerberg received a tax benefit by giving $100 million to a private educational foundation. Only a small proportion had actually been spent on education as of October 2011.[10] North American opinion has embraced Mark Zuckerberg as a public benefactor because of his social involvement, a role he clearly accepted in announcing his donation publicly on the *Oprah Winfrey Show* in 2010.[11] The story of Bill Gates's taxes is similar.

In short, someone who is clever enough to play all these tax rules in the right combination can end up as a billionaire who not only doesn't pay his or her fair share of taxes, but is also able to play a powerful role in public life.

The way our system gives power to a minority of unelected taxpayers is best illustrated by the Giving Pledge initiative. Through this initiative, a small group of billionaires will have access to $600 billion—more than half of which represents tax savings provided mainly by the U.S. government—that they can use to act on public policy questions, as they see fit. These billionaires seem to be good people, but why should societies agree to give up democratic control in this way? The democratic system is a hard-won achievement of the last few centuries, and the Arab Spring demonstrates that it remains a compelling cause in our own time.

Tax havens, tax breaks for multinationals and the super-rich, private foundations, electronic commerce and electronic money have all contributed to the fiscal gap that needs to be closed. Taken together, these developments have led to tax losses that in most countries could represent up to half the accumulated budget deficits since 2000. (See Appendix 2.)

The superrich are skilled at surfing along the fault lines of our tax systems—and doing it not just domestically but internationally. To compensate, governments are asking the rest of us to pay. The poor and the middle class, who are limited from hopping from country to country by increasingly rigid immigration rules, have little choice but to accommodate themselves to this way of doing things. Some are protesting this unjust distribution of the tax burden, in a context where a substantial and growing portion of society's wealth is concentrated in the hands of the superrich.

In January 2012, tax inequities emerged as an issue in the U.S. presidential campaign, as tidbits of information began to come out regarding the tax status of the multimillionaire frontrunner for the Republican nomination, Mitt Romney. Taking advantage of lower tax rates on investment income, Romney pays tax at a rate of only 15 per cent. In addition, Jack Blum, a Washington lawyer and authority on tax enforcement and offshore banking, commented that Romney's "personal finances are a poster child of what's wrong with the American tax system."[12]

To bring the public books back into balance, imposing austerity measures is not enough. It's also necessary to cut off the fiscal fast track reserved for the superrich. Buffett, Zuckerberg, Gates, Romney and other billionaires and multimillionaires of their ilk are not just individuals. They are products of a social system. If that social system comes up with good ideas for finding the money to balance the public accounts, it needs to be able to implement those ideas and reap a decent financial benefit from them. In addition, while Bill Gates may have made a major contribution to bringing about our current information society, the degree of wealth and power granted to him for this achievement seems out of line. Thomas Edison, who brought us electric light, wasn't granted anything close to the same privileges. Nor were Alexander Graham Bell, Marie Curie, Albert Einstein and other innovators.

The superrich are able to surf the world's tax regimes primarily because the tax regimes themselves are weak. In the twenty-first century, with its new economic arrangements and technological developments, they have become archaic and easily manipulated. The income tax, which is approaching its one hundredth birthday in most countries, has not been rethought in the current context. In current tax regimes, international coordination relies on two basic taxation principles: tax residence and source of income. These principles don't work very well in a globalized economy in which a growing number of transactions cannot easily be attributed to a specific geographic space, and where large companies can shop for tax regimes on a planetwide scale.

Because of these limitations, current tax regimes cannot generate as much tax revenue as they should from wealth accumulating in tax havens, electronic commerce, multinationals and private foundations. It's a simple mathematical proposition that if too much wealth escapes the tax system, the books cannot be balanced. If the gap, already large, continues to widen at the same speed over the next few years, tax regimes will be in crisis. Bank bailouts, stimulus programs and austerity plans have only pushed forward a problem that was already on the radar screen.

Experts knew the problem was coming. Vito Tanzi, director of the fiscal affairs department at the International Monetary Fund from 1981 to 2000, clearly predicted the possibility of fiscal crises.[13] In May 2000, when the decline in corporate income tax rates was just getting underway in most countries, an article in the *Harvard Law Review* forecast that "globalization and tax competition lead to a fiscal crisis for countries that wish to continue to provide social insurance to their citizens at the same time that demographic factors and the increased income inequality, job insecurity, and income volatility that result from globalization render such social insurance more necessary."[14]

In 2012, fiscal crises are knocking at the door, almost everywhere. Only a very small minority of countries (less than 10 per cent) still have an AAA credit rating. Greece, Ireland, Portugal and Spain have fallen into crisis several times since 2009. In the twenty-first century, fiscal crises are contagious, and since the United States was downgraded in 2011, no country is safe.

And yet, solutions *are* possible. This book explains how traditional income tax regimes have become archaic, what degree of responsibility they bear in the current fiscal crises and the ways in which many superrich individuals abuse them to avoid paying their fair share of taxes. It concludes with some proposed solutions.

I began exploring this subject in 2004 when I wrote my first book *Ces riches qui ne paient pas d'impôt* (Rich People Who Don't Pay Taxes). I never could have imagined that one day I would write a book with the title *Bill Gates, Pay Your Fair Share of Taxes...Like We Do!* But life and timing sometimes force us to say unexpected things. I chose to put Bill Gates in the title because he symbolizes better than anyone else what the current generation of tax systems has produced: a small minority of very rich taxpayers who have used the undue financial advantages the system grants them to obtain extraordinary wealth and power.

As you read this book, keep in mind that it is not the product of a political party, a newspaper, a trade union, a university, a research institute or a government. It is the result of an exhaustive and completely independent initiative on my part, not sponsored by any institution or interest group. I appreciated every step of this process, and I hope my passion for the subject will elicit the same response in you.

1

FISCAL EPIDEMIC

The economic crisis facing us today is unprecedented in history. This is the first time that so many countries around the world are simultaneously finding it impossible to balance their books as they try to confront deficits and debt loads of staggering proportions. In 2011–12, following the outbreak of the subprime crisis in the United States and the recession that followed, the world entered another period of massive financial turmoil. While there is no doubt that governments have occasionally run into serious financial trouble in the past and either adjusted or collapsed, the fiscal crises of the twenty-first century are different. With new means of communication and the globalization of trade and currencies, what might once have been isolated problems have now become an epidemic. As of now, every country is at risk.

In the nineteenth and twentieth centuries, government fiscal crises were infrequent (See Appendix 1 for a brief discussion of fiscal crises throughout history.) Countries went into debt to deal with shortfalls in their revenue. But these crises became ubiquitous in the early twenty-first century as many countries faced the harsh reality of no longer being able to borrow to keep their governments afloat. With national debt crises erupting in European Union countries, the U.S. and elsewhere, taxpayers and public authorities are entering a period when they must renegotiate the terms on which their own nation's wealth and spending are shared. If these countries and their citizens fail to find acceptable new arrangements, tax revolts are most likely to be the outcome.

A fiscal crisis—the inability of a government to raise enough tax revenue to pay for its programs and activities— typically progresses through four distinct phases, if efforts to avoid it are unsuccessful. In Phase 1, governments run a deficit which they finance through increases in the national debt. In Phase 2, as the debt mounts, governments find themselves in a crisis situation, unable to borrow funds needed to finance their deficits on acceptable terms. In Phase 3, governments have no choice but to find a new consensus among the population about how its activities are to be paid for, while in Phase 4 (reached if Phase 3 produces no satisfactory outcome), tax revolts begin to erupt.

In 2012, sovereign states around the world have accumulated debts totalling more than $47.5 trillion.[1] Most of these states are already in Phase 3 of a fiscal crisis—the stage where there is a renegotiation of the social compact between taxpayers and their governments—because they are facing a rapidly growing national debt and have no choice but to renegotiate that social pact. A few of the world's governments are still in Phase 1, yet even they are trying to establish new understandings with their citizens in an attempt to avoid a worse situation in the future.

The financial crisis of 2008 and the economic crisis that followed it have exacerbated the decline in public finances and hurt many countries' ability to borrow. Governments had to run large deficits and go deeper into debt in order to maintain economic activity and break a deflationary spiral as well as to enable banks to get rid of bad debts and households to retain their savings. As a result, fourteen out of every fifteen countries saw their public finances deteriorate in 2009–10,[2] with the world's overall government debt load rising by more than $10 trillion since 2008.[3] The financial crisis of 2008 merely aggravated the sizable deficits that some countries were running even before the crisis struck. The decline in tax revenues caused by economic slowdowns, corporate bailouts and extraordinary spending to stimulate the economy and cover the costs of wars and natural disasters are the explanations usually offered to explain these higher deficits.

Since the twenty-first century began, fiscal crises have been officially declared by the governments of Iceland, Argentina, Greece, Ireland and Portugal. At the same time revolts have occurred in many Arab countries, sparked by citizenry protesting the unjust allocation of wealth, among other things. In this sense, the crises of the Arab Spring (which turned into the Arab Year)—in countries like Tunisia, Egypt, Libya, Bahrain, Syria and elsewhere—belong to the family of fiscal crises we are discussing here.

THE CRISIS IN EUROPE IS CONTAGIOUS

One of the key problems we face today is that we are no longer immune to the financial crises in other countries. If Greece, Ireland or the United States develops a financial disease, it has the potential to infect the entire global system. There are many reasons for this new susceptibility: systemic risks in the banking and financial systems,[4] the growth of international trade and the dependence of all countries on the euro and the U.S. dollar. In 2012, only sixteen of the 126 countries examined by international rating agencies enjoyed the highly coveted AAA credit rating: Australia, Austria, Canada, Denmark, Finland, France, Germany, Işle of Man, Luxembourg, Netherlands, New

Zealand, Norway, Singapore, Sweden, Switzerland and the United Kingdom. The rest—including the United States—had ratings that indicated concern on the part of rating agencies about the financial stability and capacity of those governments.

While individual member countries like Germany, France and Austria may still be considered AAA, the European Union overall has been going through the most serious crisis in its history. This began in the spring of 2010 when Greece hit the wall after the turmoil of the 2008 financial crisis and then continued in a downward financial spiral afterwards. The Greek government tried to avoid defaulting on its debt by seeking assistance from the International Monetary Fund and the EU and by adopting austerity plans heavily tilted towards spending cuts. The most recent plan includes civil service pay cuts, job and pension cuts, a new property tax and a privatization plan (including ports, utilities and the state lottery). In a report issued on June 21, 2011, the United Nations stated that such radical deficit reduction policies threaten employment and social spending and jeopardize economic growth.[5] Greek taxpayers responded angrily to government measures, and a series of general strikes erupted. In May 2011, three people were killed when the ministry of finance and a bank were firebombed with Molotov cocktails.[6] Protests continued as taxpayers demonstrated with increasing violence. Greece was clearly at Phase 4 of a fiscal crisis.

Then it was Ireland's turn. After the 2008 recession, Ireland followed in the wake of Greece as it sought to save its banks from failure, paid benefits to thousands of unemployed workers and aided troubled companies. Prior to 2008, the national budget was balanced and the country was nicknamed the Celtic Tiger because of its stunning financial performance, but it was imperilled by a huge speculative real-estate bubble that burst in 2008, thrusting it into an unprecedented crisis. The EU and IMF launched a rescue plan, and the government adopted a draconian austerity program.

The panic spread to Portugal next. In November 2010, a rescue plan was adopted to cope with the government's debt load. Austerity measures were then applied, and large demonstrations erupted. Protesters gathered in front of houses to try to prevent bailiffs from seizing houses from their owners. In May 2011, 300,000 people gathered in Lisbon and Porto to demand a more equitable fiscal plan. In September 2011, the new centre-right prime minister, Pedro Passos Coelho, issued a warning: "In Portugal, the rights to strike and to demonstrate are inscribed in the constitution. But we cannot tolerate those who mistake the enjoyment of these freedoms for the right to torch the streets and set fire to the country."[7]

Meanwhile, in Spain the government was adopting a series of austerity measures. Like Ireland, Spain had been the scene of a speculative real-estate bubble that burst at the time of the 2008 recession. But Spanish citizens refused to bear the burden of the crisis, responding to the government's program of cutbacks with protests.

In Italy, the economy was stagnating and the country plunged into conflict. In July 2011, an initial austerity plan was adopted, with a second one following in August.[8] In September, thousands of Italians took to the streets to protest these measures, rejecting the bitter medicine being forced down their throats. The police used clubs and tear gas to disperse people demonstrating against the government's plan in front of the Senate.[9] Silvio Berlusconi, once again Italian prime minister as of May 2008, resigned in November 2011. He was replaced by Mario Monti, former international adviser to Goldman Sachs and former European commissioner.

And these countries were not alone. In 2011, Cyprus,

France and even parts of Germany were also considered to be at increased risk of a fiscal crisis. Between 2007 and 2009, the number of unemployed workers had already increased by 35 per cent in Europe. As the fiscal crisis and the resulting austerity hit, unemployment began to rise to even higher levels. This surge in unemployment coincided with an increase in the suicide rate by 13 per cent in Ireland and 17 per cent in Greece.[10]

NORTH AMERICA IS NOT IMMUNE

Like a disease that is quickly transmitted, these fiscal crises crossed the Atlantic to threaten the United States and Canada. The U.S. economy, which had already been affected by its own domestic crisis, slowed again in early 2010. For the first time since the end of the Second World War, debt exceeded 100 per cent of GDP, with economic growth declining and unemployment hitting record levels.[11] In the ten years from 2000 to 2010, U.S. federal debt jumped from $5.5 trillion to $14 trillion.

The U.S. government, divided between a Republican House of Representatives and a Democratic Senate and White House, hit a roadblock in its efforts to manage the debt and public finances. By 2011, the urgency of getting the United States out of its financial impasse was clear, but Congress proved incapable of dealing with the problem in a nonpartisan manner. The Republicans refused to raise the debt ceiling without a significant reduction in public spending.[12] Their argument was that "Washington doesn't have a revenue problem, it has a spending problem." Influenced by the Tea Party movement, the Republicans opposed tax increases that would allow "big government" to decide where investment should occur rather than letting the market determine resource allocation.

More than 95 per cent of Republican members of Congress had signed the Taxpayer Protection Pledge devised by right-wing lobbyist Grover Norquist and his organization, Americans for Tax Reform. Anyone seeking a Republican leadership position had to treat this as a sacred commitment. Signatories to the Taxpayer Protection Pledge[13] promise never to vote for a tax increase or a reduction in tax deductions or tax credits without the added revenues being offset by tax reductions. The legality of the Taxpayer Protection Pledge has been called into question by a growing number of politicians. Democratic Senator Dick Durbin said, "It bothers me because I think my first obligation is to this country and to this state, not to any individual or any political action committee."[14]

At the last minute, on August 2, 2011, President Barack Obama reached an agreement with Congress to raise the debt ceiling. The agreement called for the debt ceiling to be raised in three phases. The first step, which took effect on August 2, 2011, required public spending to fall by between $2.4 trillion and $2.5 trillion over ten years, with no mention of tax increases. The next steps left the door open to tax increases and additional spending cuts. But a few trillion dollars over ten years will not be enough to deal with the problem, at least not according to Standard & Poor's which downgraded the U.S. federal government's AAA credit rating. According to Standard & Poor's, "The budget balancing plan on which Congress and the Executive have recently agreed is insufficient compared to what, in our view, would be needed to stabilize the public debt on the medium term."[15]

The August 2 agreement officially opened the way for the United States to enter Phase 3 of a fiscal crisis. There was a strong possibility that the ensuing public debate about how the debt and national wealth ought to be shared might turn into a tax revolt, because extremists on both the right and the left could make common cause. Other factors in play were the rise of the superrich and the impoverishment of other classes, along with the alienation felt by ordinary Americans and their difficulty in understanding the highly complex and substantial issues at stake. But the Occupy movement of fall 2011 marked the beginning of a new stage in the American debate around taxes and government, with its focus on the growing gap between the rich 1 per cent and the other 99 per cent of the population. For these protesters, the message was clear: they would not pay for the errors of a system that functions for the benefit of the wealthy 1 per cent.

According to a report titled *Economic Security at Risk*,[16] published in July 2010 by the Rockefeller Foundation, the economic insecurity index of American families was at its highest level in twenty-five years. The study pointed to "the middle-class squeeze." In the first-quarter of 2012, one seventh of all Americans relied on the federal government for food aid in the form of food stamps or other government programs. Meanwhile, according to the Federal Reserve, the largest multinationals held a record $1.9 trillion in cash reserves in 2010, and the average total compensation for CEO's was $11.4 million—up 23 per cent in just one year.[17] CEOs had salaries averaging 343 times the $33,190 earned by the average American worker in 2010,[18] compared to a ratio of 42 in 1980 and 85 in 1990.

Who will come to the assistance of the United States if the fiscal crisis gets worse? The Americans are able to imagine ways of helping other countries but, unlike Greece, Ireland and Portugal, the United States cannot be saved by the International Monetary Fund or other organizations. It can be rescued only by the Americans themselves.

Canada, with an economy tightly linked to that of the United States, is not immune to a debt and fiscal crisis. Although Canada was one of the few countries still boasting an AAA credit rating in 2012, it would have to remain vigilant.

Canada lost its AAA credit rating from Standard & Poor's on its foreign currency debt in 1992, before winning it back in 2002. Ten years later, the U.S. downgrade, the European debt crisis and the threat of renewed recession seemed likely to weaken the financial position of Canada's federal and provincial governments.

In the face of this threat, Stephen Harper's government reassured the public by telling them that the Canadian banking system faced no major problems and that the unemployment rate was much lower at home than in other countries. In the 2010–11 federal budget, Finance Minister Jim Flaherty also explained that the Canadian debt-to-GDP ratio of 33.9 per cent was well below the worldwide average[19] (of 59.9 per cent in 2011[20]).

This comparison was misleading, however, because it did not take provincial debt into account. When this is added in, the debt-to-GDP ratio rises to more than 85 per cent, putting Canada among the highly indebted countries, with a per capita debt of $39,000 in 2012.[21] Any assessment of the risk of a crisis in Canada needs to consider the fiscal fragility of its provinces. Quebec's gross debt reached, for example, $173 billion in 2011, representing 55 per cent of its GDP,[22] and it faces substantial challenges related to the aging of the population and the increase in health care costs. As of 2012, Standard & Poor's was giving Quebec an A+ credit rating. This was the grade given to Italy until September 2011.

Canada's 2011 federal budget declared that the Harper government would use austerity measures to balance the budget by 2014–15 (in November 2011, Finance Minister Jim Flaherty announced that balancing the budget would have to wait until 2015–16[23]). It would continue to detax—that is, lower tax rates of—large corporations,[24] although the budget also suggested that the government would add $1 billion a year in tax revenues by closing some loopholes. This was not an ambitious objective. In 2011, the Organisation for Economic Co-operation and Development (OECD), the organization of mostly rich countries, estimated that Canada could have collected additional billions of dollars if it had eliminated certain tax advantages that it provided to corporations in 2008.[25]

Should a debt crisis occur in Canada, there is every reason to believe that Canadian taxpayers would strongly oppose drastic austerity plans. Middle-class Canadians seem to have the impression that they are already heavily taxed, with too high a public debt and an inability to contribute more. In Quebec, the 2010–11 provincial budget was a turning point, with 12,000 taxpayers demonstrating in Montreal (and others elsewhere) under the theme *"La richesse existe! Prenons-là où elle est!"* ("Wealth exists! Take it where it's found!"). This was a response the budget's higher income and consumption taxes and increased fees that were to be borne essentially by the middle class. The Occupy movement and other protest movements proved surprisingly strong. In the fall of 2011, Canadians were prepared to sleep outside all winter to show how serious their struggle was.

OTHER COUNTRIES ARE ALSO SUSCEPTIBLE

Prior to 2008, Iceland was among the world's most developed countries, ranking first in 2006 by the Human Development Index.[26] But the world economic and financial crisis hit Iceland with the impact of a meteorite. The country's three main banks, comprising nearly the entire banking system, went into receivership in October 2008. Rather than adopt the "too big to fail" approach favoured by the U.S. and European Union, Iceland opted for a "too big to save" strategy. The oversized dimensions of its banking institutions, with assets equal to ten times the national GDP, left it no other choice.[27] The Icelandic government indemnified local customers but left 340,000 British and Dutch citizens who had deposited funds in the banks high and dry. On their own initiative, the governments of the United Kingdom and the Netherlands then indemnified their own citizens. Since then, these two governments have been demanding €3.8 billion from Iceland to pay for this measure. But ordinary Icelanders sent a clear message to their own government: they would not pay for the failure of private banks. Icelanders rejected two reimbursement proposals presented in referendums in March 2010 and April 2011.

While European countries that were victim to the debt crisis imposed a series of unpopular austerity plans in 2011, Iceland, which chose to let its banks fail, was gradually emerging from the crisis. Exports rose, household debt was renegotiated and extended, unemployment stabilized at between 8 and 9 per cent and economic growth resumed in the middle of 2010.

Economists offer three reasons to explain how this tiny economy—Iceland has only 320,000 inhabitants—was able to emerge from the crisis in better shape than other countries. The first reason was its "too big to save" approach. The second was the devaluation of the Icelandic króna: the currency fell 40 per cent in late 2008, and aluminum and fish exports grew as a result. Not being part of the euro zone, Iceland was able to use devaluation as a measure to stimulate economic activity—though it cost consumers who had to pay much more for imported goods. The third reason was that its austerity measures were less severe than elsewhere.[28]

The crisis has also affected Britain, where austerity has been met with vigorous protests. In the fall of 2011, the British government launched a ten-year, £30-billion (€35 billion, $47 billion) infrastructure program to counterbalance the negative effects of its austerity plan, which it has refused to soften. In late October 2011 unemployment was at 8.3 per cent, or 2.64 million in absolute numbers—the highest number Britain had seen in seventeen years.[29]

Japan, the third largest economy in the world (China is now number two) has the largest debt burden of any industrialized country, at about 200 per cent of GDP. The principal causes are the persistent deflation and slow growth that have affected Japan for years. Even though Japan has not yet shown signs of following Greece, Ireland and others into fiscal crisis, pressure is on the government to finally put in place a credible plan to balance the budget and contain its debt levels.[30] Meanwhile, the BRICS countries (Brazil, Russia, India, China and South Africa) are doing better. Their share of the world economy is growing rapidly: from 16 per cent of global GDP in 2001 to 27 per cent in 2011 and, according to some estimates, to 40 per cent in 2025.[31] In this period of turbulence, the relative importance of the BRICS countries has grown. However, while there was no risk of an immediate crisis in these countries, they were concerned about their financial and economic dependence on countries where the risk of a crisis is much greater.

Many countries face major challenges in terms of public finances, and they must be prepared for financial turbulence in the coming years as they adjust to this new century. In addition to dealing with current crises, the world's population is growing by eighty million each year, aggravating problems of unemployment, pollution, waste, epidemics, water supply, famine, deforestation, desertification and depletion of nonrenewable resources.[32] In many industrialized countries, the population is aging, and spending on pensions and health care is likely to rise sharply in the coming years—unless cutbacks force lower living standards on the retired and the sick.

According to the U.S. Congressional Budget Office, government spending on health care represents the greatest long-term fiscal problem for the United States. It accounted for 5.3 per cent of GDP in 2010 and was expected to climb to 10 per cent in 2035 and 19 per cent by 2082.[33] David M. Walker, U.S. comptroller-general from 1998 to 2008, has noted, "If there is one thing that could bankrupt America, it's health care costs."[34] In Canada, Old Age Security and Guaranteed Income Supplement payments were expected to quadruple (or double after taking inflation into account) between 2009 and 2036.[35] When it comes to health care, total spending exceeded $191 billion in 2010.[36] Two thirds was provided by provincial and territorial governments. With an aging population, provincial health care costs could be ranging between 9 per cent and 12 per cent of GDP by 2036.[37]

In the United States in March 2011, the bipartisan Committee for a Responsible Federal Budget hosted an event in Washington financed by the MacArthur Foundation, focusing on the human side of the fiscal crisis. One of the panels dealt with the high cost of inaction for vulnerable future generations and individuals.[38] It was argued that if political authorities did not become more proactive, these vulnerable groups would be the victims of the fiscal crisis. "The U.S. fiscal house is in trouble," the panel's report stated:

> *Even now, our government cannot provide goods*
> *and services to the American public at current*
> *tax levels without resorting to heavy borrowing.*
> *The situation will only get worse in the future, as*
> *the average age of our population increases from*
> *the double whammy of lower birth rates and the*
> *retirement of the Baby Boom generation. The*
> *aging population will need more government*

services but, at the same time, tax contributions won't keep pace with spending, because growth of the working-age population will slow. For programs like Social Security, which will have to depend on a lower number of workers making contributions for a larger number of retirees, the aging of the population has real consequences.

CUT SPENDING OR RAISE TAXES?

Confronted with the threat of a fiscal crisis and faced with investors' concerns about the ability of governments to repay their debts, countries need to find solutions for balancing their books. As we saw earlier, the solutions instituted up to now by most governments and international organizations have consisted of austerity plans with a primary focus on public spending cuts, which have created harmful effects felt mainly by the middle class and the poor. Various plans have been imposed by the International Monetary Fund, the World Bank and the European Commission, under threat of sanctions.[39]

Viewed early in the crisis as a necessary evil to deal with past excesses, austerity plans were initially accepted. The story is different today. It has become harder for taxpayers to accept austerity plans, whose negative effects—lower incomes, unemployment, insecurity—have become visible, while the hoped-for results have not materialized. Many taxpayers have found it unjust to ask the poor and the middle class to make sacrifices even though the increase in the public debt was mostly due to the rescue of private banks during the financial crisis of 2008. Taxpayers today have no interest in picking up the tab for mistakes that were made by others. In Europe, opponents have shouted a traditional slogan loudly and clearly: *"Cette crise nous ne la paierons pas!"* ("We're not paying for this crisis!"). Indignation has been brewing like a gathering storm, and demonstrations are picking up strength.

Poor and middle-class taxpayers lack the financial ability to withstand public spending cuts. According to recent figures from the U.S. Census Bureau, 14.3 per cent of Americans were living below the poverty line in 2009, a rise of 13.2 per cent over 2008.[40] In Canada, according to a Conference Board study, about 12 per cent of the labour force was living in poverty in 2009.[41]

What is clear from these figures is that the situation is dire in many countries. The economic crisis has become an almost perpetual subject of debate—and yet, in the midst of all the discussion, one key point has often been missed. It is impossible for governments to balance their books by relying solely on spending cuts. The deficit is simply too great, and as a simple matter of mathematics, it is unrealistic to believe that spending cuts alone can succeed in salvaging government coffers. David Stockman, U.S. budget director during the Reagan era, said in an interview on April 11, 2011: "It is simply unrealistic to say that raising revenue isn't part of the solution. It's a measure of how far off the deep end Republicans have gone with this religious catechism about taxes." Simon Johnson, economic counsellor and research director at the International Monetary Fund in 2007 and 2008, says a 50/50 approach between spending cuts and revenue increases should be followed.[42] A Washington Post-ABC News poll on June 9, 2011,[43] found that 61 per cent of Americans believed that higher taxes would be needed to balance the government budget.

This inability to balance the books through spending cuts suggests that the current crises have a hidden face, and that there is a fundamental problem on the revenue side. Revenues in various industrialized countries have been falling rapidly not just since the 2008 financial crisis erupted but since the start of the twenty-first century. Between 2000 and 2009, tax receipts in the United States fell from 29.5 per cent to 24 per cent of GDP while spending rose from 33.9 per cent to 39 per cent of GDP[44] during the same period. In Canada, tax receipts fell from 35.6 per cent of GDP in 2000 to 32 per cent in 2009.[45] Austria, Belgium, Denmark, Finland, France, Germany, Greece, Iceland, Ireland, Israel, Luxembourg, the Netherlands, Slovakia, Spain, Sweden, Switzerland and the United Kingdom have also had to deal with lower receipts. This downward trend is a first since 1965 (when the OECD began compiling its statistics), and provisional results for 2010 showed an even sharper decline.

The basic problem is that tax systems that were devised nearly a hundred years ago are no longer adequate in the twenty-first century. Under the OECD Model Tax Convention, which inspired the tax conventions ratified by Canada and most other industrialized countries, international tax coordination relies on two basic taxation principles: tax residence and source of income. How are these principles applied in a globalized economy? Today, an ever-growing number of operations are hard to attribute to a specific geographic space. At the same time, multinationals and superrich individuals are free to shop around the globe for the tax system that suits them best. This is the current reality: tax systems are incapable of taxing the wealth that is accumulating in tax havens and private foundations and changing hands through electronic commerce. Yet in the end, it is a matter of simple mathematics—if too much wealth escapes the tax system, the books can no longer be balanced.

In recent years, a number of leading experts have warned governments that a fiscal crisis was looming, explaining clearly that the growing popularity of new phenomena such as tax competition, tax havens, e-commerce and so on has made traditional tax systems archaic.

In May 2000, with corporate tax rates beginning to fall in various countries, a working paper published in the *Harvard Law Review* warned that "globalization and tax competition lead to a fiscal crisis for countries [like Canada] that wish to continue to provide social insurance to their citizens at the same time that demographic factors and the increased income inequality, job insecurity, and income volatility that result from globalization render such social insurance more necessary."[46] Finishing his twenty-year stint as director of the IMF's fiscal affairs department in 2001, Vito Tanzi issued this warning to tax administrations:

> *Globalization and the consequent international integration, together with rapid technological progress, is likely to affect both the ability of countries to collect taxes and the distribution of the tax burden...Most industrial countries are collecting more tax revenue today than they did two or three decades ago. On closer inspection, however, one can detect what may be called "fiscal termites" gnawing away at the foundations of their tax systems...Faced by these termites, as well as by others that may yet appear in the future, many countries, particularly those with high tax rates, would be advised to prepare for what could be sharp declines in tax revenues.*[47]

Among the "termites" Tanzi listed were electronic commerce, electronic money, offshore financial centres and intracompany trade. Meanwhile, Michael J. Graetz, professor of tax law at Columbia Law School, said,

These fundamental rules for accomplishing and enforcing international tax policy were put in place during the formative period—1918 through 1928—for international income taxation, a time when the world economy was very different. Recent years have witnessed, for example, the rise of e-commerce, the expanded use of financial derivatives, the invention of e-money, the increased mobility of capital, a rise in the use of tax-haven financial centres and more sophisticated cross-border legal and financial arbitrage, all of which have helped render archaic (or easily manipulated) the longstanding core concepts used worldwide to implement international income tax arrangements and policies."[48]

These archaic tax rules have provided for the creation of a growing wealth bubble that escapes taxation, making it extremely challenging to balance public accounts.

Taken together, these tax shortfalls could represent up to half the accumulated budget deficits since 2000 in many countries.[49] Since tax shortfalls will just keep growing over the coming years, it is unlikely that we can resolve our fiscal crises by relying solely on spending cutbacks, and it would be unjust to try to do so.

LOWERING TAX RATES FOR THE WEALTHY

Between 1913 and 1980, developed countries established progressive taxation,[50] with the top marginal tax rate exceeding 90 per cent in the United States from 1944–1956. But the growing influence of neoliberal economic thinking in the mid-1970s began to undermine the consensus around progressive tax rates on the grounds that they deterred wealth creators. This school of thought had many champions in the 1980s and 1990s, including British Prime Minister Margaret Thatcher and U.S. President Ronald Reagan. More recently, it found an aggressive advocate in U.S. President George W. Bush. The end result is that the top marginal tax rates on the superrich in the United States fell from 91 per cent in 1960 to 35 per cent in 2012.

Western Europe also followed this trend. In France, a three-year plan to cut taxes by 100-billion francs (€15 billion) was announced in the summer of 2000. The amendment of income tax rates in 2005 reduced the progressive nature of income tax rates by awarding 40 per cent of the tax cuts to the wealthiest 10 per cent of the population.[51] Finally, the notorious "tax shield," a mechanism implemented in 2005 to cap the total percentage of a household's income that can be taxed, resulted in 834 of the wealthiest taxpayers each receiving refundcheques in 2008 for €368,261 on average.[52]

In eastern and central Europe, income tax rates also became much less progressive. Some countries, like the Czech Republic, Slovakia, Romania and Bulgaria, even adopted flat taxes— single-rate income taxes with no real progressive dimension.

A diminishing proportion of the world's "superwealth" is subject to estate tax. This tax has not existed in Canada since the 1980s, nor in Italy since 2002. George W. Bush attempted to eliminate it in the United States. In France, it applies in theory, but in practice it has not amounted to much since 2007. The disappearance of the estate tax makes it easier to transfer wealth between generations and deprives governments of a potentially important source of revenues.

In Canada, the effective tax rates applying to the wealthiest 0.01 per cent who file personal income tax fell from 71 per cent in 1943 to 33 per cent in 2000 (including both federal and provincial taxes, with provincial rates averaged).[53] In 2011, the effective rate was probably well under 30 per cent—nowhere near the average statutory rate of 48 per cent. *The Rise of Canada's Richest 1%*,[54] a study issued by the Canadian Centre for Policy Alternatives, shows that the wealthiest Canadians managed to grab 32 per cent of all income growth between 1997 and 2007, in part through the decline in the progressive nature of income taxes.

In the United States, 63 per cent of the wealth produced since 1979 has gone to a small group consisting of the richest 10 per cent of Americans. The superrich 1 per cent of this group took 38.7 per cent.[55] In China, according to the U.S. firm Bain & Company,[56] the number of wealthy citizens reached 585,000 in 2011, double the number in 2008. In France, incomes of the top 0.01 per cent of earners increased by 40 per cent on average between 2004 and 2007, from about €900,000 to €1.27 million in declared income per person per year.[57]

Economic systems were not expected to lead to these excesses of wealth. No Nobel Prize in economics has been awarded for imagining a system where there would be billionaires on the one hand and billions of people surviving on a dollar a day on the other. Progressive income tax rates are important because they are an effective means of redistributing the excess wealth concentrated in the hands of a small minority.

Taxation of the superrich has been a live issue in a number of countries—notably in the United States where Democrats have pressed the issue strongly. A McClatchy-Marist poll conducted in April 2011[58] found that 64 per cent of American voters—and even 45 per cent of Tea Party supporters—were in favour of raising taxes on the wealthy. Alan Greenspan, chair of the U.S. Federal Reserve from 1987 to 2006, stated on April 17, 2011, that it would make no sense to reduce the deficit significantly if high-income people did not contribute to the effort.[59] Between 2001 and 2007, 66 per cent of the proceeds of economic growth went to the wealthiest 1 per cent of the U.S. population.

On August 15, 2011, the *New York Times* printed an open letter from billionaire investor Warren Buffett criticizing the way in which the wealthiest Americans were able, through a series of exemptions, to pay tax at below-average rates.[60] Buffett pointed to himself as an example, noting that in the previous year he had paid taxes equal to only 17 per cent[61] of his taxable income while people working in his investment firm paid an average of 36 per cent. "My friends and I have been coddled long enough by a billionaire-friendly Congress," he wrote. "It's time for our government to get serious about shared sacrifice" to balance the budget. After his letter was published, a number of other superrich people around the world also suggested that their governments raise their income taxes, asking to be more heavily taxed as a sign of solidarity with all citizens at a time of crisis.

In Canada, where problems of public finance have been less acute than in the United States or Europe, the undertaxation of wealth is not a hot-button issue. If financing the debt becomes a problem, though, or if other countries start taxing the superrich much more heavily, it is unlikely that Canada will be able to escape this debate.

HOW TO CREATE A FISCAL HOLE

Chapter 2 of this book looks at the detaxation of multinational corporations. Globalization has eliminated many barriers to international trade, but obstacles to human migration still exist. This is the reason why financial capital has become more mobile than human capital. Multinationals can set up shop wherever it suits them, targeting countries with generous tax systems, and creating fierce tax competition in the process. Countries are constantly cutting their corporate tax rates—by an average of 40 per cent in OECD member countries during the last twenty years and from 32.6 per cent to 25.4 per cent between 2000 and 2011.[62] Greece cut its rate by half, from 40 per cent to 20 per cent, between 2000 and 2011. In Canada, corporate tax rates have fallen by nearly half, from 29.1 per cent in 2000 to 15 per cent in 2012.

Advocates of corporate detaxation generally assume that these rate cuts do not jeopardize the country's public finances because they are offset by greater commercial activity and higher taxable income. In their view, corporations will invest the money they save through lower taxes in expanding their businesses. With this broader tax base, the corporate contribution to government finances should rise even if the actual tax rate comes down. Recent OECD statistics suggest that this assumption is simply wrong.[63] Greece has had to cope with a 40 per cent drop in the amount contributed to its public finances by corporate taxes. In Canada, the substantial decrease in corporate tax rates between 1975 and 2008 led to a drop of one quarter in the proportion of income taxes paid by corporations, from 14 per cent in 1975 to 10.4 per cent in 2008.

Chapter 3 examines tax havens. New means of communication and greater capital mobility help taxpayers easily get around the principle of tax residence by establishing (or pretending to establish) their tax residence or income source in countries that are tax havens. A report published in 2008 by a U.S. Senate subcommittee showed that tax fraud in offshore tax havens was costing Americans $100 billion a year. In that same year, eighty-three of the 100 biggest American companies had subsidiaries in tax havens. A study published in March 2010 by Global Financial Integrity showed that total deposits held by nonresidents in offshore financial centres and tax havens totalled about US$10 trillion. As a point of comparison, total worldwide GDP was $71 trillion.

Chapter 4 delves into electronic commerce. Traditional taxation principles that were devised more than half a century ago were based on a physical world, with tangible goods, and defined places of business where employees went to work. In the virtual world, goods that were once tangible—books, for example—have become intangible, and cyberspace is where consumers and merchants meet. Tax laws and system administrators lose their bearings, and the public treasury loses out on billions of dollars. When a Canadian connects to a server located in India to buy goods made in China from a company based in Luxembourg, it is difficult for the Canada Revenue Agency to tax the income arising from the sale.

In Chapter 5, I look at private foundations. Contrary to popular belief, private foundations are not a good deal for public finances in the short or the medium term. A foundation has to spend only 3.5 per cent of the value of its assets for charitable purposes each year. (This figure is 5 per cent in the United States.) Generally, foundations have no desire to spend more than their return on capital because their founders seek to conserve the initial capital. Governments thus have to wait more than twenty years to begin seeing their money. In Canada, wealth totalling more than $20 billion was tied up in private foundations in 2010, and in the United States, the figure was more than $600 billion.

Chapters 6 and 7 deal with possible approaches to solving the fiscal crisis. Chapter 6 deals specifically with environmental taxation. If major fiscal reforms are to be undertaken to deal with the crisis, this could be a strategic moment to implement a green tax shift. However, green taxation options need to be considered very carefully, and I examine some of the problems involved in implementing green taxation, in Canada and abroad. In Chapter 7, I look at a broader range of tax reform proposals to address the major sources of the tax shortfall.

FISCAL COUP

The ineffectiveness of tax systems in the twenty-first century creates a problem that goes well beyond numbers and the undermining of public accounts. In addition to not paying their fair share of taxes, the superrich, through the strategic use of the various forms of tax leakage made possible by an archaic system, are able to become disproportionately influential. Take Mark Zuckerberg and Facebook, for example.

In October 2008, three years after going live, Facebook moved part of its operations to Ireland. It's not clear what is left in the United States, but Ireland seems to play an important role in the organization.[64] Among OECD countries, Ireland is a well-known tax haven. It seeks to benefit from tax rates that are much lower than those in the United States and from a very favourable tax regime for revenue realized from intangible properties. And nearly all of Facebook's wealth is intangible. Assuming that Facebook had a value of $2 billion in 2008[65] and $100 billion as of 2012,[66] it is fair to conclude that this decision to involve Ireland in the corporate structure allowed the organization to save billions of dollars.

A few months later, Facebook founder Mark Zuckerberg developed a taste for philanthropy. He transferred some small bits of this wealth to a private foundation. Zuckerberg announced in September 2010 on the *Oprah Winfrey Show* that he would donate $100 million[67] to create Startup: Education, a private foundation—in exchange for generous tax credits. The donation was to be directed to the public school system in Newark, New Jersey.[68] According to a report in the Washington *Post*, only a few million dollars of this amount had actually been donated to the education system as of November 2011.[69]

By surfing the weaknesses and loopholes of the world's tax systems to avoid paying what is generally considered "a fair share of taxes," Zuckerberg has managed to earn himself the title of greatest philanthropist of his generation. At age twenty-eight, he was named *Time* magazine's Person of the Year in 2010 and was listed as the ninth most powerful person on the planet by *Forbes* magazine.

But perhaps the most striking example of billionaire-turned-philanthropist is Bill Gates, cofounder of Microsoft and chair of its board of directors, whose personal fortune is estimated at $56 billion as of March 2011[70] and $59 billion in November.

It is well known that Microsoft went to Ireland, where the tax regime on intellectual property is extremely advantageous, to set up its patent management subsidiary.[71] In this instance, the intangible portion of income earned can be quite substantial. Transfers of Microsoft patents are recorded as part of the Gross Domestic Product of Ireland, but Irish citizens don't really see this money. The beneficiaries of these tax strategies are mainly Microsoft shareholders, starting with Bill Gates himself. With Ireland at the edge of the financial abyss, the American Chamber of Commerce Ireland, of which Microsoft is a member, warned the government against raising taxes, threatening that companies might pull out of the country in the future.[72]

To get revenues out of Ireland, Microsoft uses other countries—frequently the Netherlands and Barbados—and a little tax trick called "Double Irish" or "Dutch Sandwich." At the end of the road, this lets the company park its revenues outside the United States almost tax-free.[73]

Over the years, Microsoft's tax surfing has been global in scope. According to its most recent annual report (June 2011),[74] the company has accumulated $44 billion in "permanently reinvested earnings" outside the United States. The annual report also estimates the income taxes payable when those earnings are repatriated to the United States at $14 billion,[75] amounting to 31 per cent of the $44 billion held outside the country. To avoid double taxation, the United States allows corporations to deduct foreign taxes paid, so the difference between this rate of 31 per cent and the U.S. statutory rate of 35 per cent represents taxes already paid by Microsoft in other countries. In other words, we can deduce that, through an array of tax techniques, Microsoft pays tax at a rate of only 4 per cent on its foreign profits.

With the financial difficulties faced by the U.S., Gates recently said that he is "generally in favour of the idea that the rich should pay somewhat more,"[76] but meanwhile, in Washington lobbyists were actively promoting a repatriation tax holiday that would enable this sizable stash of Microsoft's profits to be brought back to U.S. soil almost tax-free![77]

Private foundations form the final piece of Gates's tax strategy. In exchange for generous tax advantages, Gates established the Bill and Melinda Gates Foundation and transferred part of his wealth to it.[78] But it has not escaped notice that the control of the foundation seems to be in the hands of Bill and Melinda Gates[79] and it is administered to preserve its capital in perpetuity. To this end, the foundation[80] keeps its capital intact, tax-free, and rarely spends more than its return on capital for charitable purposes.

To celebrate Gates's largesse, *Time* magazine named him its Person of the Year in 2005, along with his wife Melinda, and Bono, the singer from U2. Gates was also named a Knight Commander of the Order of the British Empire for his contribution to British business and for his efforts in fighting world poverty. He was the world's fifth most powerful person in 2011, according to *Forbes* magazine. Then, in November 2011, Gates called on the G20 countries to increase their assistance to poor nations.[81]

Gates and Zuckerberg, Microsoft and Facebook are examples of success that the system has made possible. It seems reasonable to ask them to give something back by simply paying their fair share. Most of the countries where Microsoft, Facebook and others like them operate are high-tax countries where the average corporate rate is well above what they are paying.

The demand for reform is becoming increasingly urgent. It is time to put an end to an archaic tax system that allows high-net-worth individuals to polish their images around the world and wield public influence while other taxpayers foot the bill. We should be sending a clear message to Gates and his billionaire buddies. The message should be: "Pay your fair share of taxes like every other taxpayer and leave issues of public policy to the people who were elected by our democracies." As long as governments continue to ignore this situation, they are complicit in the fiscal crises we face and in a transfer of control that is threatening our democratic system.

2

TAX BREAKS FOR MULTINATIONALS

n 1907, future U.S. President Woodrow Wilson said, "Since trade ignores national boundaries and the manufacturer insists on having the world as a market, the flag of his nation must follow him, and the doors of the nations which are closed against him must be battered down. Concessions obtained by financiers must be safeguarded by ministers of state, even if the sovereignty of unwilling nations be outraged in the process."[1] Today's supporters of globalization advocate the total opening of markets in order to allow the magic of the profit motive to operate without economic barriers. While Wilson appealed to national interests in support of open markets, current advocates of globalization use economic doctrine to justify their position.

In a perfectly globalized world, the entire earth becomes the locus of competition. To survive in this environment, companies must generate "satisfactory" profits. Therefore, according to its supporters, globalization provides for optimal use of resources: only the most gainful forms of production survive, and this can only be to the advantage of every human being.

In a free-market context, countries must attract and

retain businesses. They have various means of doing this. Low-cost skilled labour and a favourable tax system are a winning combination. High-quality infrastructure and access to particular natural resources also have an influence on where transnational companies choose to go. Success tied to the opening of markets (like the powerful rise of the Chinese economy) gives weight to the ideology of globalization.

But this doctrine has some glaring weaknesses. For example, with the world becoming a global village, economic turbulence in one country is felt in many countries, as recent financial crises have shown. In something akin to a domino effect, the crisis eventually envelops the entire world economy.

The negative local effects of globalization also seem to have been overlooked. On January 28, 2009, in a news conference at the Economic Policy Institute in Washington,[2] Robert Cassidy, a senior Clinton-era official who managed U.S.-China trade relations, made a surprising assertion. He expressed the view that globalization had greatly harmed Americans. Chinese membership in the World Trade Organization was having very damaging effects on the American people, he said: fewer job opportunities, less economic stability and, above all, less income for the government and for U.S. citizens.[3]

Another flaw in pro-globalization ideologies is the great difficulty countries face in aligning their tax systems with this new economic reality. In a world free of economic obstacles, multinationals can shop around for tax systems and choose the country offering them the most favourable tax rates. Over the years, this dynamic has sent countries careening into fierce competition and has caused dramatic declines in tax rates applying to multinationals.

As we shall see, the decline in corporate tax rates—let's call it "corporate detaxation"—results in the weakening of public finances and an extra burden on other categories of taxpayers, revealing a crucial flaw in how globalization is currently oriented. It may not be possible to turn back the move to globalization, but some means must be found of ensuring that the financial health of government is protected and that the tax burden remains equitable for the majority of people.

CORPORATE DETAXATION

In the 1980s, top statutory corporate income tax rates were rarely less than 45 per cent. By 2000, the OECD average rate had fallen to 32.6 per cent. In the last decade, tax competition has intensified even further under the sway of increased mobility for multinationals, and the OECD average rate was only 25.4 per cent in 2011. According to the OECD, "This trend seems to be widespread, as rates have been reduced in 31 countries and increased only in Chile (from 15 to 17 per cent) and Hungary (from 18 to 19 per cent)."[4]

In Canada, this rate has dropped by nearly half, from 29.9 per cent in 2000 to 15 per cent in 2012. If corporate detaxation continues at its current pace, there is reason to believe that this "race to the bottom" will result in the total detaxation of large companies within a few decades.

In the May 2007 issue of the *OECD Observer*, one author notes that "if the linear trends in the OECD countries are extrapolated into the future, statutory corporate tax rates will hit zero by the middle of this century."[5] The American Enterprise Institute for Public Policy Research, a powerful right-wing think tank that was founded in 1943 and strongly influenced the neoconservative policies of the Bush Jr. administration, came to a similar conclusion on the thirtieth anniversary of its *Tax Notes* in 2002: "Accordingly, absent successful attempts at tax harmonization, it seems unlikely that the corporate income tax will exist when this fine journal assembles its sixtieth anniversary issue."[6]

Despite current or future crises in the public finances of various industrialized countries, governments continue moving towards tax reductions for multinationals. In Canada, the Harper government aims to balance the budget by 2015–16, relying on austerity, while continuing the process of detaxing large corporations whose rates have been lowered from 16.5 per cent in 2011 to 15 per cent in 2012. In Ireland, after three years of recession and in the face of tax dumping accusations from the European Union and more particularly from France, the government continues its fierce defence of its corporate tax rate of 12.5 per cent, one of the lowest among OECD countries. In the words of the late Brian Lenihan, who was minister of finance from 2008 to 2011, it is better to tax the Irish population heavily than to run the risk of losing everything by causing international capital to flee.[7] In Greece, before the debt crisis that gripped the country, the government had promised corporations that they would get additional tax cuts which would gradually lower their tax rate to 20 per cent between 2010 and 2014. Despite a crucial need for cash and the very obvious importance of corporate income tax for public finances, Greece announced on September 12, 2010, that it would accelerate the tax cuts pledged to companies, which could then benefit from the reduced 20 per cent rate starting in 2011.[8] At the time of this announcement, Greek Prime Minister George Papandreou stated, "Either we'll win together or we'll sink together."[9]

With corporate tax rates lowered, governments will face severe challenges balancing their budgets. In addition to the tax cuts already provided in the last fifteen years and the unfair competition from tax havens, multinational corporations also benefit from generous tax credits and deductions, and often from tax holidays under which they are exempted from corporate income tax for several years after they have set up shop—enough time, it is hoped by governments, to build their loyalty.

However, it is not easy to make multinationals loyal. The case of computer giant Dell shows the power of multinationals and their indifference towards host countries. In 2008, Dell announced the closing of its plants in Ireland and their relocation to Poland, creating panic on the Emerald Isle. At least 1,900 jobs were eliminated, and when Dell's suppliers were also taken into account, there were 10,000 jobs gone in the Limerick region.[10] Dell had gone to Ireland to take advantage of the preferential tax regime offered to large corporations. For nineteen years, this site was the company's leading edge, with record productivity. The European Globalisation Adjustment Fund injected 23 million in retraining funds and aid for self-employment to help workers recover from Dell's departure.[11]

In Poland, meanwhile, the situation was just the opposite. Łódź became a boomtown. Following the collapse of the textile industry, this industrial city of 700,000 inhabitants launched a vast program aimed at attracting foreign investors. The Dell plant was set up alongside the Bosch and Gillette plants in the special economic zone adjacent to the city. Dell received 54.5 million in assistance from the Polish government to help it set up in Łódź—nearly one quarter of the total investment planned by the American firm at that site. In December 2008, the European Commission ordered a detailed investigation of whether this subsidy would distort competition. Nine months later, in a press release, the commission announced that it "has authorised, under EC Treaty state aid rules, 54.5 million of regional aid, which the Polish authorities intend to grant to Dell Products Poland for the establishment of a manufacturing plant in Łódź (Poland)."[12]

ARGUMENTS IN FAVOUR OF CORPORATE DETAXATION

Despite the visible harm caused by tax competition between governments, arguments are sometimes advanced to defend it. In a 1956 article titled "A Pure Theory of Local Expenditures,"[13] the economist Charles Tiebout argued that tax competition is not harmful because, on the one hand, governments offer a combination of taxes and services and, on the other hand, taxpayers can "vote with their feet"—in other words they can go where the combination of taxes and services suits them. According to Tiebout, this competition would induce governments to reach for the best overall tax-and-service combination. The main flaw in this reasoning is that it is based on unrealistic assumptions about taxpayer mobility; in the twenty-first century, financial capital has become far more mobile than human capital, and the vast majority of individuals lack any real possibility of settling where tax pressures are lower.

Since Tiebout's article, other arguments have been advanced in favour of tax competition. Some suggest that in a world where perfect competition and the free flow of capital prevail, corporate detaxation could be advantageous for governments. In this idealized economic model, a company is just a production intermediary, and taxing it is of no use to government financing because, in the final analysis, shareholders, employees and customers are the ones paying taxes. Governments could thus save time and money by leaving companies alone. One question comes out of this suggestion: who ultimately pays corporate income tax—shareholders, customers or employees? Assuming that companies stopped paying tax, the answer to this question is crucial in conveying the corresponding tax burden to the right group of taxpayers. Box 1 sums up the various schools of thought. Economists are divided on this issue, and coming up with a firm answer seems impossible.

Another argument in favour of corporate detaxation sees the inevitable lack of standardization in how companies are taxed (both within and between countries) as an added factor of local and international economic distortion. At the local level, the favourable treatment given to certain companies because of their size can effectively hold back the natural growth of their competitors and, accordingly, the optimal use of a country's resources. At the international level, the distortions are even greater since the choice of jurisdiction in which to set up a multinational's head office and production and distribution facilities is directly influenced by tax policies.

Who Pays for Corporate Taxes?

The advocates for corporate tax cuts argue that corporations are just intermediaries, and pass on taxes to others, and thus there is no point in taxing corporations. Is it really that simple?

Shareholders: The advocates for corporate tax cuts argue that shareholders ultimately pay when corporations are taxed. Corporate taxes will reduce the ability of a corporation to pay dividends to investors, or will reduce share prices, or both. However, in an era of globalization, capital is mobile; often shareholders live in another jurisdiction. If the government doesn't tax such a corporation, it is exporting revenues to another country.

Employees: The advocates argue that corporate income taxes reduce the ability of companies to reinvest in improving their production tools, as well as in training, development and so on. This results in lower employee productivity and, thus, lower ability to pay employees. However, if the alternative to taxing corporations is to tax employees, then employees will likely earn even less, in after-tax income. Also, corporate profits are closely linked to employee productivity. In an era of new technologies, skilled labour is in high demand, and companies have to offer attractive compensation in order to retain skilled employees. They cannot allow themselves to simply convert corporate taxes into lower wages.

The advocates also argue that corporate taxation encourages corporations to move to places with lower taxes, resulting in employees losing their jobs (and thereby paying for corporate taxes). However, packing up and moving isn't entirely free of costs; moving farther from suppliers or markets raises transportation costs. And skilled workers are scarce; the corporation will need to pay to recruit and train new employees, or pay for them to be relocated.

Customers: Advocates point out that corporations will attempt to pass on costs, including taxation costs, to customers to the extent possible. The theory of corporate taxation being passed on to consumers was first advanced in the seventeenth century by economist Sir William Petty. He argued that consumers end up paying higher prices for goods and services from companies that are taxed. However, with the opening of global markets, the ability to raise prices is limited, as firms risk being crushed by competitors based in lower-cost countries. This makes it harder for such corporations to pass on taxes to consumers.

REASONS NOT TO ENGAGE IN CORPORATE DETAXATION

In practice, no country operates in the idealized economic context that advocates of detaxation use as a reference model. Some of the eight main reasons why governments should avoid corporate detaxation arise directly from taking this real-world complexity into account. Others, however, would remain pertinent even in the advocates' fantasy world of pure and perfect competition. Here are the arguments:

The first reason not to engage in corporate detaxation is that the taxes not paid by corporations will have to be covered by other groups of taxpayers. As we have seen, however, economists do not agree on who ultimately pays corporate taxes now (see Box 1). So if governments detax corporations, they may be engaging in wealth transfers between shareholders, employees and customers.

A second reason is predictability of revenues. Corporate taxes provide for the immediate taxation of corporate income. With corporate detaxation, the point at which tax becomes payable on that income depends on when the corporation transfers these amounts to shareholders. This can create serious difficulties for public finance.

Another reason is that the favourable treatment provided to corporations would tempt many taxpayers who would not normally have considered it to form companies and "incorporate" themselves. This would put an even heavier tax load on individuals. Those who did not incorporate—because they are unaware of the tax advantages, because of the costs involved or, more often, because it cannot be done in their area of work—would have to bear part of the tax burden that their "incorporated" fellow citizens ought to be handling. (Governments would seek to maintain a certain level of tax receipts, but there is also a chance that their overall revenues would fall.)

A fourth reason is that corporate taxation digs into "superprofits"—the profit margin exceeding what economists regard as "normal profits." What this means is that corporate tax, which skims off a portion of a company's surplus, is not very painful for the company but does constitute a necessary source of revenue for government and respects the principle of a degree of equity among various social players in sharing the tax burden.

Another reason relates to the widespread practice of targeted detaxation. It is equitable to tax all companies, multinationals and small businesses alike. However, governments often give preferential tax rates to certain companies, based on their sector or size. Detaxing one type of company—whether large or small—and continuing to tax others is unfair.

A sixth reason relates to the trend towards detaxing large multinational corporations in order to attract them to a particular jurisdiction. Detaxing multinationals gives them an unfair advantage over new entrepreneurs and boosts their ability to control world markets. There are signs that something like this may already be happening. Many products in stores with different brand names, appearing to come from competing manufacturers, are in fact all produced by the same multinational. In democratic capitalist societies, if this situation is regarded as undesirable, governments should take care to avoid detaxing multinationals.

A seventh reason is that companies should not be allowed to benefit from public services without contributing to them. Whether calculated in absolute terms or as a percentage of GDP, corporate income tax is declining. However, just like other economic players, companies need governments and their various services. We should recall that, when a multinational chooses to set up shop in a country, this choice is influenced by a range of factors other than tax treatment, including quality of infrastructure and labour, access to natural resources, quality of the legal system and so on.[14] It seems logical and fair that these key elements should not be offered to companies free of charge, with other taxpayers having to make up the costs. In many cases, some employees of large corporations are not citizens of the host country and are not taxed there. It is even more unfair for income tax to be paid neither by employees nor by employer, even though they benefit from the use of public services.

An eighth reason, and there might be others, is that corporate detaxation does not guarantee that financial capital will be attracted. Corporate detaxation may be a valuable tool in attracting multinationals to some countries, but for other countries, such as Greece, Portugal and Canada, detaxation would not produce a systematic rise in foreign investment. On the contrary, Canada's corporate tax rate fell from 28 per cent to 21 per cent between 2000 and 2006, but even so it experienced a decline in foreign investment.[15]

Furthermore, because of international tax rules, tax cuts in one jurisdiction could be recouped by taxes on that corporation in another jurisdiction. International taxation often involves a "treasury transfer": in most OECD countries, international tax rules apply the principle of taxing residents on the basis of their worldwide incomes and providing credits for taxes paid abroad. According to these rules, a foreign multinational that receives a dividend from its Canadian subsidiary should ultimately be taxed according to the higher of the two effective rates—the rate in its home country or the rate in Canada. Thus, even if Canada lowers its tax rates, a multinational's overall tax load could end up being just as high. The tax credit provided by the home country would be reduced accordingly, and the tax payable in that country would go up. Canada would then suffer a loss of revenue without enjoying a rise in foreign direct investment: its lowering of taxes would thus benefit other countries.[16]

In a Department of Finance research report issued in 2008,[17] the Canadian government recognized that lowering tax rates could lead to a loss of revenue to the benefit of other jurisdictions, but it played down this factor. It explained that U.S.-based multinationals (representing 50 per cent of foreign investment in Canada) may use tax-planning techniques so as to repatriate their Canadian income to the United States without paying more in U.S. taxes. Canada's tax reductions would thus continue to be of interest to them. In other words, Ottawa was defending its tax policy by arguing that multinationals will attempt to dodge taxes in their country of origin. This illustrates a key point in tax competition: it is often a "race to the bottom," in which corporations and their shareholders benefit while the public loses tax revenues.

Finally, taxation is not the only criterion that multinationals look at when choosing where to operate. They also consider other criteria such as the services provided by the country, employment conditions, the political situation, language and so on.

THE IMPACT OF CORPORATE DETAXATION ON REVENUE

Arguments against corporate detaxation would be incomplete if we failed to mention the biggest problem it creates: loss of revenue.

According to recent OECD statistics, business corporations accounted for an average of 11 per cent of the budgets of member countries in 2007.[18] Canada and the United States sat right at the OECD average, with ratios of 11 per cent in that year.[19] Considering the financial importance of the corporate income tax in government budgets, could abolishing it jeopardize countries' public finances?

In May 2007, the *OECD Observer* answered this question by stating that "without action, we could be on the verge of a global tax crisis that could hurt economic activity. The tax burden cannot be carried by labour and consumption alone. The upshot of inaction would be a loss of revenue for governments and a downward spiral in economic activity."[20] In May 2000, as noted, as corporate tax cuts got under way, the *Harvard Law Review* warned that "globalization and tax competition [will] lead to a fiscal crisis for countries that wish to continue to provide social insurance to their citizens at the same time that demographic factors and the increased income inequality, job insecurity, and income volatility that result from globalization render such social insurance more necessary."[21]

In Canada, advocates of corporate detaxation generally assert that lower tax rates do not jeopardize countries' public finances because they will be offset by increases in economic activity and hence in taxable income. However, *offsetting* doesn't mean that corporations would continue to pay *as much* in Canada after taxes are cut.

Recent OECD statistics[22] shed some light on the impact of corporate tax cuts. Between 1975 and 2008, as a result of Canada's sizable corporate tax cuts, the proportion of income taxes paid by corporations to support the country's public finances declined by a quarter, from 13.6 per cent in 1975 to 12.2 per cent in 2000 and to 10.4 per cent in 2008. A similar trend can be seen in other countries. For example, the corporate contribution to the tax base fell by 35 per cent in Finland, 40 per cent in Greece, 20 per cent in the Netherlands and 15 per cent in Ireland, Luxembourg and the United States between 2000 and 2008.

Until recently, fiscal crises were avoided in most countries—first because their economies were growing and their tax bases were expanding even as tax rates fell, and second because the resulting shortfall could be made up by raising countries' debt levels or workers' tax loads. But these compensatory measures appear to be reaching their limits. In Canada, the share of public finances covered by personal income tax rose from 22 per cent in 1965 to 37 per cent in 2008—a 70 per cent increase.[23]

In a number of countries, further increasing the public debt has become harder to envisage. The financial crisis in Greece illustrates this clearly. Greece's public debt was 165 per cent in 2011,[24] The IMF has projected it to hit 189 per cent in 2012, and even if everything goes according to plan, Greece's public debt-to-GDP ratio will still exceed 120 per cent in 2020.[25] Back in 2006, the CPB Netherlands Bureau for Economic Policy Analysis had predicted that big corporate tax cuts could seriously damage the economy in Greece, which had lowered its rates by more than a third, from 40 per cent in 1996 to 25 per cent in 2007.[26] These reductions caused the share of corporate tax in Greece's public finances to tumble by half.[27]

THE KEY TO STABILITY: BALANCE

The checklist for keeping a country running smoothly is quite long, but it could be shortened to a few basic rules. For example, it is generally recognized that raising the standard of living of a country's inhabitants goes hand in hand with the development of savings, capital accumulation, education, technology and infrastructure. A major drawback to corporate detaxation is that it jeopardizes the basic rule that, to optimize the running of a country with a market economy, some balance needs to be maintained between the powers of government, markets and citizens. Otherwise, the system reacts and attempts to reestablish a balance on its own.

During this adjustment period, a country does not use its resources optimally, and this hurts its inhabitants' well-being. For example, if government is more powerful than citizens, the result will be dictatorship. In the opposite case, if citizens become more powerful than government, there is anarchy. And so on and so forth. The only case where the outcome has yet to be known is when market rules beat out government rules. This is what is happening now in most industrialized countries. *Business Week* magazine commented back in 1995 that "in this new world market...billions can flow in or out of an economy in seconds. So powerful has this force of money become that some observers now see the hot-money set becoming a sort of shadow world government—one that is irretrievably eroding the concept of the sovereign powers of a nation state."[28]

Government versus market: this test of strength is as old as the modern state itself. Thomas Jefferson, the third United States president, issued a warning against the rising power of financiers: "I hope we shall crush in its birth the aristocracy of our moneyed corporations which dare already to challenge our government to a trial of strength and bid defiance to the laws of our country."[29] Since the 1980s, the power struggle between the two camps has tilted in favour of high finance with the rise of neoliberalism in politics and the argument that wealth creation is stronger when government steps out of the way and leaves the road open to private initiative. Zbigniew Brzezinski, a founder of the Trilateral Commission in 1972 and national security adviser to President Jimmy Carter, was clear about this: "People, governments and econ-omies of all nations must serve the needs of multinational banks and corporations."[30]

This was a credo that scarcely troubled much of the Western political class until the major financial crisis of 2008 came along and called it into question. Post-neoliberalism is perhaps already underway, and the balance between markets and government may perhaps be readjusting. We may be living through one of those moments when, as Italian philosopher

Antonio Gramsci said, "the old is dying and the new cannot be born." Failing this, if the current trend continues, we will reach a situation in which corporate "citizens" push the entire tax burden onto actual human citizens with the very powerful ones gaining control over the governments. We could end up with a new form of slavery.

Irrespective of the theories for or against it, corporate detaxation runs the risk of being viewed by public opinion as favouritism. A large majority of taxpayers see multinationals as entities that generate huge profits for the benefit of wealthy shareholders who clearly have the wherewithal to pay taxes. For social peace to be maintained, it seems that this group needs to pay at least minimal taxes. Supporters of corporate detaxation hope to support their position through an information campaign, even if the economic theory they use as a justification is open to challenge—as strikingly illustrated by the absence of a straightforward answer to the question of who really pays corporate taxes. What wage-earners tend to understand very clearly, however, is that they are the ones who have to make up for the government shortfall. In Canada, income tax paid by individuals rose from $18 billion in 1975 to $190 billion in 2008.[31]

After the pros and cons have been weighed, an understanding of corporate reality in the era of globalization leads to the conclusion that corporate income tax is essential to the tax system in the twenty-first century. Governments may allow themselves to be charmed by the rhetoric of the corporate detaxation hawks, but the flaw in their reasoning cannot be ignored forever. Corporate detaxation is not only unjust, but it is also harmful to every group concerned: shareholders, employees and consumers alike.

3

HAVEN FOR THE RICH, HELL FOR THE REST OF US

The time when tax havens consisted of exotic islands where a few gangsters or corrupt dictators hid their fortunes is long gone. Tax havens have become sanctuaries for an array of multinational firms and their subsidiaries or corporate parents. They form part of the background to most of the financial crises and scandals of the last twenty years. "Madoff Spotlight Turns to Role of Offshore Funds," ran a *New York Times* headline on December 30, 2008. It had taken just nineteen days after Bernard Madoff's $65 billion swindle broke into the open on December 11 to draw the link between the swindle and tax havens.[1]

Since the financial crisis of 2008, politicians' attitudes towards tax havens have changed. Government leaders now recognize that tax havens endanger public finances and their countries' political stability. The OECD is stepping up the fight against international tax fraud and, increasingly, promoting international tax transparency. At the London G20 summit in April 2009, countries announced the advent of a new era of transparency and tax cooperation.[2]

Despite these advances, the problem remains unresolved. Trillions of dollars continue to accumulate beyond the reach of government in tax havens, with the middle class left to fill the public coffers and make up for this shortfall. As protesters outside the G20 summit at Cannes, France, in November 2011 called for an end to tax havens, officials of the G20 inside issued a list of eleven countries, including Switzerland, that they said were doing too little to cooperate.[3] However, no sanctions were announced.

WHAT IS A TAX HAVEN?

According to a study published in December 2006 by the U.S. National Bureau of Economic Research,[4] about 15 per cent of countries around the world are tax havens. Most of these countries appear to be financially well off and are relatively small in size.[5] Few OECD member countries have precise definitions, though. Most see tax havens as states with systems enabling nonresidents to shirk tax obligations to other governments, along with bank secrecy.

The OECD uses three criteria to determine whether a country is a tax haven: absence or near-absence of income taxes; absence of transparency in the tax system; and a refusal to exchange financial or tax information with other governments. The OECD added the third criterion because, taking account of only the first two, countries with tax systems that offer tax-free zones or highly generous tax advantages in certain regions or for particular areas of activity could wrongly be viewed as tax havens.

In addition to tax havens, there are three other types of haven-type zones. In *offshore zones* that are home to banks, insurance companies or fund managers but lack a true financial regulatory apparatus, companies can avoid various restrictions by having addresses only in these states. Then there are *bank havens*, states characterized by a high level of bank or financial secrecy. Finally, there are *judicial havens*, which evade criminal and other laws generally adopted by other states and refuse any exchange of information with other states.

Some may be multihaven zones, falling into more than one of these categories. Strictly speaking, a tax haven differs from the three other types, but in practice these distinctions are often blurred. It is not uncommon for offshore zones to be regarded as tax havens.

WHERE ARE THESE TAX HAVENS LOCATED?

In *Global Political Economy: Contemporary Theories*,[6] Ronen Palan, professor of international political economy at the University of Birmingham, separates tax havens into two geopolitical poles. The first group gravitates around the London financial centre, mainly encompassing dependencies of the British Crown such as the Isle of Man, the Channel Islands of Jersey and Guernsey, the Cayman Islands, Bermuda, the British Virgin Islands, the Turks and Caicos and Gibraltar, as well as former parts of the British Empire such as Hong Kong, Singapore, Malta, the Bahamas, Bahrain and Dubai. The other group developed around economic activities in the rest of Europe and includes the Benelux countries (Belgium, the Netherlands and Luxembourg) together with Ireland and, of course, Switzerland and Liechtenstein. Two other tax havens, Panama and—to a small extent—Uruguay, operate independently of these poles.

Each year, the OECD draws up a list of uncooperative tax havens. In 2000, the OECD identified thirty-eight such entities, including Andorra, Anguilla, Antigua, Aruba, the Bahamas, Bahrain, Barbados, Belize, Bermuda, the British Virgin Islands, the Cayman Islands, the Cook Islands,

Dominica, Gibraltar, Grenada, Liberia, Liechtenstein, the Marshall Islands, Monaco, Montserrat, Nauru, the Netherlands Antilles, Niue, Panama, Saint Kitts and Nevis, Saint Lucia, Saint Vincent and the Grenadines, Samoa, San Marino, the Turks and Caicos Islands and Vanuatu.

In 2009, in coordination with the G20 summit, the OECD published a new listing of tax havens divided into four categories, depending on the level of noncooperation (white, pale grey, dark grey and black). The white list encompasses jurisdictions that have broadly applied a standard of transparency and information exchange. This standard involves an obligation to exchange information on request in all taxation-related areas for the administration and application of national tax laws.[7] The two grey lists cover tax havens and financial centres that have made commitments concerning this standard but have not yet applied it. To go from a grey list to the white list, countries must sign at least twelve agreements with other countries. Finally, the black list consists of jurisdictions that have not agreed to apply the internationally recognized tax standard.[8] As of December 15, 2011, there weren't any countries on the black list and just three on the two grey lists (Nauru, Niue, Guatemala).[9]

These results are surprising. It is not as if there is any reason to believe tax havens are disappearing. In one year, tax havens such as Liechtenstein, the Cayman Islands, Monaco, the Bahamas, Bermuda and Singapore ended up on the white list by signing most of their information exchange agreements among themselves.[10] At the very least, it is too early to judge the effectiveness of the recently signed agreements, the application of which will be subject to meticulous follow-up by the Global Forum on Transparency and Exchange of Information for Tax Purposes. We will take a closer look at this body's role further on in this chapter.

WHAT ARE THE RESULTS OF TAX HAVENS?

Tax havens cause harm to countries that are not tax havens, which suffer deterioration of public finances, increased financial instability and injustice. Let us take a closer look at each of these problems.

The existence of tax havens leads to capital flight from non–tax havens, which are deprived of taxes they would otherwise collect as companies move head offices or activities to tax havens. On January 5, 2010, Canada's then-Revenue Minister Jean-Pierre Blackburn stated that Canadian companies and individuals had a total of C$146 billion invested in tax havens in 2009, a substantial increase from the $88 billion total in 2003.[11] These amounts are just approximations. Whether at the national or international level, nobody has yet managed to put an exact figure on the scale of revenues lost to tax havens. But there are some credible estimates.

- A study published in March 2010 by Global Financial Integrity, a Washington-based international organization that works to curtail illicit financial flows, estimates the total amount deposited by nonresidents in offshore financial centres and tax havens at about US$10 trillion (for the sake of comparison, annual worldwide GDP in 2010 was $74 trillion[12]). The study also states that these deposits are growing by an average of 9 per cent a year, substantially more than the rate of increase of worldwide wealth in the last decade.[13]

- According to the October 2007 report *Offshore Explorations: Jersey*, published by Tax Analysts, a U.S. tax policy organization, "At the end of 2006, there were $491.6 billion of assets in the Jersey financial sector beneficially owned by non-Jersey individuals who were likely to be illegally avoiding tax on those assets in their home jurisdictions. We estimated the comparable figure for Guernsey to be $293.1 billion."[14] If we add $150 billion in investments in the Isle of Man, as estimated by Tax Analysts in a November 2007 report, we get assets totalling $935.2 billion in these three islands alone.[15]

- In March 2005, the Tax Justice Network, a pressure group that opposes tax havens, published a report titled *The Price of Offshore*.[16] According to this study, the total of large private fortunes held in tax havens was about $11.5 trillion, producing an annual return of about $860 billion (at a rate of 7.5 per cent) and a $255 billion loss of tax receipts. These figures do not take into account tax losses resulting from the multinationals' offshore tax strategies or transfer costs or assets below $1 million held by individuals. Rates of return were probably less than 7.5 per cent in recent years, but international capital markets have grown substantially in that time.

- A report issued on July 16, 2008, by a U.S. bipartisan Senate Permanent Subcommittee on Investigations estimated that offshore abuses cost U.S. taxpayers an estimated $100 billion each year.[17] And again, that study did not consider the public revenues that are lost by industrialized countries because of tax strategies of the multinationals in tax havens.

- An analysis produced for Oxfam in March 2009 by James Henry, former chief economist of McKinsey & Company,[18] suggests that at least $6.2 trillion from

developing countries is held by individuals in offshore
accounts, depriving these countries of $64 billion
to $124 billion annually in tax receipts. Total losses
may thus exceed the $103 billion these countries
receive annually in development assistance. And if
the amounts held by private companies in offshore
accounts were included, this shortfall would be much
higher. Henry indicates that this capital flight from
developing countries is growing quickly, with an
additional $200 billion to $300 billion moving into
offshore accounts each year.

It should also be noted that tax havens cause a deterioration of public finances in non–tax havens by exposing them to
fierce tax competition. Because of the existence of tax havens,
other countries are tempted to reduce their tax rates to attract
new investment or retain companies already established on
their territory. In Canada, the federal government is planning
substantial tax reductions for multinational corporations. In
2012, Canadian multinationals were to be taxed at a legal rate
of 15 per cent at the federal level (or a total of about 25 per
cent a year with provincial tax added), compared to 35 per
cent in the United States (to which must be added the corporate taxes applied in certain states). This sharp decline gives
reason to wonder whether Canada is seeking to become a tax
haven. On June 29, 2009, the Tim Hortons fast-food chain
surprised Canadians and Americans alike when it announced
it was moving its main place of business from Delaware—
known as a tax haven in the United States—to Canada.

The opaque nature of tax and banking havens prevents
fiscal, judicial and financial authorities in other countries from
enforcing laws and regulations. Free from requirements to
publish statistics, financial statements and other information,

multinationals can place dicey assets outside public scrutiny and hide the origin of funds. These veritable black holes are obviously valuable to transnational criminal organizations as well.

This opacity also leads to significant errors in trade and financial statistics. It disconnects a country's real economy from what shows on the books, depriving governments and investors of information they need to assess risks and make the right decisions. For example, going strictly by public information, one would learn that Europe's largest importer of bananas is the tiny island of Jersey, off the coast of Normandy, but in fact no containers of bananas have ever been unloaded in the port of Jersey.

The rate of return on projects conducted through tax havens is artificially inflated, giving them sizable benefits compared to projects that have to deal with tax authorities. The opacity provided by tax havens thus increases distortions in capital markets. Billions of dollars end up being invested in high-risk projects with fictitious advantages. This situation can magnify financial crises and create a domino effect.

A wide array of events proves that the presence of tax havens lurks in the background of the 2007–10 financial crisis. For example, the failed British bank Northern Rock charged its short-term debt to Granite, a Jersey-based subsidiary.[19] An investigative report by McClatchy News in 2009 showed how the investment bank Goldman Sachs used the Cayman Islands to promote $40 billion in AAA-rated junk securities to private and institutional clients. This was how Goldman Sachs got rid of all the subprime mortgages it held shortly before their value collapsed in 2007. At the same time, the bank was speculating on the markets by taking short positions on these same securities. Goldman Sachs used its Cayman Islands branches to promote these securities without having to comply with U.S. regulations, which would have required it to warn its clients that it was using its own money to bet against its customers.[20]

Tax havens have appeared in the background of nearly all the financial crises, megafrauds and business scandals of the last twenty years, including the southeast Asian crisis of 1997, the Russian crisis of 1998 and the bankruptcies of the energy broker Enron in 2001, the food giant Parmalat in 2003 and the financial services company Refco in 2005.

The first form of injustice caused by the existence of tax havens arises from the fact that it creates a two-tier international tax system: one tier for ordinary people and another for the rich. Tax havens are used by the wealthy and the powerful to hide wealth and avoid taxes. They help shape a certain type of globalization in which the gap between the very wealthy and everyone else keeps growing. A report titled *Unfair Advantage: The Business Case Against Overseas Tax Havens*,[21] issued in July 2010 by the American group Business and Investors Against Tax Haven Abuse, shows that "overseas tax havens foster an unlevel playing field where small and domestic U.S. businesses that pay taxes are forced to compete against tax dodgers." For example, "Wainwright Bank, a socially responsible local lender based in Boston, paid 11.8 per cent of their income in federal taxes in 2009. Yet they have to compete against Bank of America, which paid no federal taxes in 2009, thanks in part to overseas tax havens."

The second form of injustice tax havens create is that they facilitate abuse by multinational firms of the natural wealth of undeveloped or developing countries. Jersey's bananas are an example of this. These bananas, transiting virtually through Jersey, generate untaxed profits that accumulate in the accounts of multinationals. These untaxed profits should go in part to the southern countries, which unfortunately are the main victims of such stratagems, seeing their bread and butter disappear in tax havens.

In 2008, OECD secretary-general Angel Gurría said that developing countries lose huge amounts to tax havens—three times what they get in assistance from developed countries.[22] Similarly, it is noteworthy that African countries not only are being shaken by a financial crisis that they are in no way responsible for creating but must also deal with the failure by industrialized countries to pay the amounts pledged in connection with the Millennium Development Goals.

A third form of injustice caused by tax havens is the way they lead citizens and tax authorities to bend and possibly break laws. The HSBC-2010 and Liechtenstein-2008 affairs are examples.

In the HSBC-2010 affair, Hervé Falciani, a former bank executive with HSBC in Geneva, was arrested by the Swiss police on suspicion of data smuggling. He took refuge in France and helped authorities decrypt the stolen data.[23] France opened a money laundering investigation and used the information obtained from Falciani to identify the alleged fraudsters. France then shared its information with other countries, including Canada.[24] In response to the ensuing criticism, French President Nicolas Sarkozy said, "The fight against tax fraud is normal and moral. It is up to the justice system to say what happened. But what would you have said if the finance ministry had disregarded these data when it received them? Would we have been congratulated for abiding by French law?" He added, "I support the ministry in its action against fraud."[25]

The Liechtenstein-2008 scandal involved taxpayers from various countries, including Germany, France, Australia, the United States and Canada, who had transferred funds to trust accounts in Liechtenstein with the complicity of banks such as LGT Bank, owned by the Liechtenstein royal family. In February 2008, computer technician Heinrich Kieber sold financial data that incriminated 4,500 taxpayers to the German government for €4.2 million.[26] The German government was criticized for using secret information stolen by an informer.[27] Two lawyers took action against Germany's federal government for "infidelity toward the taxpayer" and "spying of data." Questions were raised as to the legality and ethics of the government's move in paying a bribe to an officer of a foreign bank to essentially steal confidential data.

In September 2010, the Canada Revenue Agency (CRA) stated that files from the HSBC affair would be analyzed one by one and that aggressive action would be taken to recover money owed to Canadians. An item by The Canadian Press in September 2010 noted that various Canadian clients had confessed and that the department was seeking to encourage voluntary disclosures. In December 2010, at a hearing of the House of Commons Standing Committee on Public Accounts, Lucie Bergevin, director general of the Audit Professional Services Directorate in the CRA's Compliance Programs Branch, stated that audits had begun but officials were still analyzing the information obtained and determining what was missing.

Regarding the Liechtenstein affair, Jean-Pierre Blackburn, then Canada's minister of revenue, said on December 14, 2008, that he had a list of 108 Canadian taxpayers who had applied tax stratagems in Liechtenstein through the Royal Bank of Canada. Appearing before the Commons Standing Committee on Finance in December 2010, Lucie Bergevin stated that "we had already conducted twenty-six audits by the spring. Up to October, we conducted thirty audits. We are continuing with the audits. We have obtained good results following the twenty-six audits, namely $5.8 million."[28]

HOW TAX HAVEN PLANNING IS DONE

Using new means of communication, and aided by e-commerce and capital mobility, residents of countries with high rates of taxation may easily establish, or pretend to establish, their tax residence or income source in tax havens. Here are the main ways this is done.

The first way is by holding assets. A trust or corporation is set up in a tax haven to hold assets (usually portfolios of securities or real estate assets), normally administered by a resident of another tax haven. This stratagem means, in essence, that the nominal owners of these assets are not residents of a highly taxed country, enabling them to escape the tax burden that would apply to the real owner. This method is very popular. In Ireland and Switzerland, for example, total assets of these various subsidiaries work out to about $4.5 million per employee of the corporation. In Barbados, it comes to $22 million per employee, and in Bermuda to more than $45 million per employee.[29]

A common tool for holding assets in a tax haven is the use of international business corporations (IBCs). These are companies that guarantee the owner's anonymity, with no reporting requirements and a registration fee of about $500. There are 500,000 IBCs in Hong Kong and more than 60,000 in the Cayman Islands.[30]

Another way is by exporting commercial activities. Many companies (or portions of companies) that do not require a specific geographic location or qualified staff are set up in tax havens. Common examples are insurance or reinsurance (secondary insurance) companies with head offices in Bermuda. Others include various financial corporations, Internet-based firms and companies in the oil industry.

For example, *Deepwater Horizon*, the oil rig that exploded in the Gulf of Mexico on April 20, 2010, was registered in a tax haven. The *Deepwater Horizon* rig was leased by BP but remained the property of Transocean, an offshore drilling contractor. Transocean moved its country of registration from the United States to the Cayman Islands in 1999 and from there to Switzerland in 2008. Transocean justified its decision by the need to "improve our ability to maintain a competitive worldwide effective corporate tax rate."[31]

The growing scope of intangible assets within companies facilitates the use of these stratagems. According to a study published in March 2007 by the consulting arm of Ernst & Young, intangible assets accounted for more than 60 per cent of the value of Europe's 100 largest corporate groups.[32] And it is relatively easy to justify the location of patents, copyrights, rights to the use of logos and the like in tax havens. In these cases, to export income to tax havens, all that is needed is to show that the offshore company is the entity legally holding the right to exploit these invisible assets. We have thus seen Microsoft, pharmaceutical firms Pfizer and Bristol-Myers Squibb and telecoms giant Vodafone relocate invisible assets and intellectual property to Dublin.

An article on the Bloomberg news wire in October 2010 reported that Google Inc. had reduced its tax payments by nearly $3.1 billion since 2007 and brought its international taxation rate down to a record low of 2.4 per cent. This tax optimization was made possible by a legal technique commonly called "Double Irish," which apparently is open to various large companies in the technology sector, such as Microsoft, Apple and IBM. In Google's case, its use relies on an agreement with the U.S. tax authorities on the transfer price of intellectual property. It enables Google to benefit from a lower tax rate provided these profits are not repatriated to the United States.[33]

A third way is through financial intermediaries. Much of

the economic activity in tax havens consists of financial services provided by mutual funds, hedge funds, life insurance companies and pension funds. Funds are usually deposited with an organization set up in a tax haven that serves as an intermediary and are then invested, most often in the original highly taxed jurisdiction. Although such stratagems do not normally allow taxation to be avoided in the taxpayer's main jurisdiction, they enable suppliers of financial services to offer multijurisdictional products without adding an extra layer of taxation.

EFFORTS TO OVERCOME THE SCOURGE OF TAX HAVENS

OECD and G20: In 1977, the OECD set up a working party on tax avoidance and evasion that has a particular interest in refining the Model Tax Convention to facilitate information exchanges and removing political obstacles to them. Banking secrecy for tax purposes came under scrutiny in a report on access to bank information issued by this body in 2000. A Model Agreement on Exchange of Information in Tax Matters was reached between the OECD and certain non–OECD member countries in 2002. Since then, this model has served as a basis for several agreements on exchanges of tax information worldwide. This led, in 2004, to the first major revision of the OECD's Model Tax Convention, specifying that banking secrecy should not constitute an obstacle to the exchange of information.[34]

Following the HSBC and Liechtenstein affairs and the recent financial crisis, the issue of transparency and information exchange to fight tax evasion has been the focus of new activity. As already mentioned, the London G20 summit in April 2009 took a major step in the fight against tax havens.[35] The standard of transparency and information exchange developed by the OECD is now approved by all the main players.[36]

In 2009, the Global Forum on Transparency and Exchange of Information for Tax Purposes approved a process of peer examination that was set to last three years. Without exception, all members of the Global Forum and all jurisdictions listed by the Global Forum must be examined in two phases. Phase 1 assesses the quality of each jurisdiction's legal and regulatory framework on information exchange. Phase 2 focuses on practical implementation of frameworks. The Global Forum's ultimate aim is to ensure that international standards of transparency and information exchange for tax purposes are instituted, and that they operate effectively.

In April 2011, the forum had already issued reports on a number of its members. It was expected that, by 2014, all of its more than ninety members will have gone through Phase 1 and Phase 2 examination. Canada was one of the first countries to be scrutinized by the forum, and this examination found that the elements for effective information exchange are in place. The forum produces recommendations for improving access to ownership information involving bearers' and proxies' shares.[37]

In the late 1980s, the OECD and the Council of Europe developed a Convention on Mutual Administrative Assistance in Tax Matters. This convention encourages international cooperation in stepping up application of national legislation while respecting taxpayers' basic rights. It promotes all possible forms of administrative cooperation between governments in setting and collecting taxes. It was presented to the G20 summit in Cannes, France, in November 2011 and signed by the governments of all the G20 member states.[38]

The European Union has emerged in the last few years as the real leader in the worldwide fight against tax havens, especially through its Code of Conduct and its savings directive.

The Code of Conduct for Business Taxation, in force since 1998, provides an informal method of regulation that is much appreciated by member governments. This code is not a legally binding instrument, but it clearly has political backing. The countries adopting it agree to eliminate various harmful practices in tax competition and prevent new ones from arising. The goal is to ensure that all tax rules are applied uniformly to each firm in a country, whether national or foreign.

The savings directive,[39] in force since 2005, provides that income from savings in the form of interest paid in one country to a resident of another country is taxed effectively in accordance with legislative provisions in the country of residence. To this end, there are rules favouring the automatic exchange of information between governments.[40] Since this directive does not cover corporate entities or trusts, it can be circumvented by creating a trust in Jersey, for example.

It is worth mentioning that the EU provides a way to overcome tax barriers faced by companies that operate in more than one member country in its Internal Market: companies can be taxed on the basis of a Common Consolidated Corporate Tax Base covering all their activities in the EU.[41] In this way, a group's profit would be taxed only once in the EU, and the proceeds would be divided among the countries based on an agreed-on criterion (for example, the amount of capital invested or total sales), as is the case in the United States and between Canadian provinces.[42]

The EU had set itself a deadline of 2008 to come up with a directive on corporate taxation. But Irish voters' rejection of the Lisbon Treaty in a referendum on June 12, 2008, motivated in part by the threat it posed to the Irish tax system, delayed the project.[43] On March 16, 2011, the EU finally produced its directive.[44] It aims for a sizable reduction in administrative burdens, compliance costs and legal uncertainties faced by companies in the EU in complying with various national systems in establishing taxable profits. The common corporate tax base would enable companies to use a one-stop scheme for their tax statements and consolidate the profits and losses they record throughout the EU. Member countries will fully retain their sovereign rights in setting corporate tax rates.

In the United States, Barack Obama has seemed determined to deal with the problem. In 2005, while still a senator, he supported the Stop Tax Haven Abuse Act. One of the U.S. government's key tools is the qualified intermediary ("QI") program. QI status is a special standing given by U.S. tax authorities to banks worldwide enabling them to buy and sell U.S. securities for foreign investors. In exchange for this, they agree to provide the Internal Revenue Service with information on all income credited to American taxpayers who have accounts with them and, above all, to collect tax for the IRS by withholding up to 30 per cent at source on dividends or interest from these investments.[45]

In March 2010, the United States adopted foreign account tax compliance legislation that will oblige all financial institutions to reveal to the IRS the identity of all clients of American nationality. Clients who refuse to reveal their identity will face the automatic withholding of 30 per cent of income from these investments.[46] In most cases, withholding will begin on or after January 1, 2014.[47] The legislation has a far more extensive area of application than the QI system and will involve more members of the public in an attempt to cover all foreign financial institutions and not just the traditional sector of deposit-taking banks. It is important to note that the foreign account tax compliance legislation will not replace the existing QI system but will form a parallel system operating alongside the existing one.

Like other jurisdictions, Canada has instituted rules targeting the advantages that accrue to users of tax havens. The key measures that have been taken are: rules to manage the transfer price of goods and services transacted between related parties (e.g. corporations and subsidiaries); restrictions on the deductibility of expenses; imposition of a deduction at source when payments are made to beneficiaries living in tax havens; rules for taxing income from a company or trust established in a tax haven and controlled by a resident of a highly taxed country; imposition of a departure tax when an individual, company or trust ceases to reside in Canada; and compulsory disclosure to the authorities of improper tax planning in which tax havens play a prominent role.

Canada is a member of several international organizations and forums that are collaborating to end international tax avoidance, including the OECD working group on information exchange and tax rule observation, the Global Forum on Transparency and Exchange of Information for Tax Purposes, the Joint International Tax Shelter Information Centre and the seven-country working group on tax havens. In the 2007 federal budget, Finance Minister Jim Flaherty stated that his government would crack down on those who avoid paying corporate income tax by intensifying the fight against the use of offshore tax havens. Canada has asked countries that are not signatories to a convention to reach an agreement on exchanging tax information within five years of a request by Canada to do so.[48] If a territory accepts such an agreement, corporate income earned in the territory by foreign companies affiliated with Canadian companies will be exempted from Canadian income tax. Otherwise, the income will be taxable in Canada as earned. Canada was negotiating tax information exchange agreements with various territories.[49] Among those signing deals with Canada have been the Bahamas, Bermuda and the Cayman Islands.

Despite these positive actions, Stephen Harper's government seems ambivalent about tax havens, and some of its decisions have received mixed reviews. Its 2010–11 budget contained a measure making it possible for Canadian taxpayers to avoid tax on profits from the sale of shares in Canadian companies.[50] This measure makes it easier for Canadian taxpayers to avoid taxes on the sale of Canadian shares by having them held through an intermediary residing in a tax haven. Meanwhile, the Canada Revenue Agency had been fighting Canadian taxpayers in court in efforts to enforce this newly abolished rule.

Alain Deneault, holder of the Canada Research Chair in Globalization at Université du Quebec à Montréal, argues that Canada sent a strange signal to the international community when it signed a free trade agreement with Panama. In an article published by the Centre for Research on Globalisation, he wrote,

> This agreement may seem inconsequential, but this is not the case. The country's main economic activity consists of offering financial services to drug traffickers and multinationals. Capital enters Panama and leaves with no restrictions. Transactions are protected by bank secrecy, so much so that there is no control of financial activity...The agreement between Canada and Panama will facilitate the illicit activities going on in that country while backing its laissez-faire approach. Whereas the G20 gathered in London

> *in 2009 had emphasized the importance of*
> *attacking the problems caused by tax havens,*
> *Canada is acting in the opposite way and*
> *opening a new front to facilitate tax leakage.*[51]

The various advances enumerated here have reduced the extent to which fraud and tax evasion are protected. However, the problem remains, and tax havens have not truly been challenged. It is necessary to go further, and to act more quickly.

4

SHOPPING WITHOUT BORDERS

Tax regimes date from a time before electronic commerce was a reality. Traditional principles of taxation were based on a physical world of tangible goods, a defined place of business and people who worked there. In the virtual world, where assets are intangible and merchants and consumers meet in cyberspace, these principles have lost their foundation.[1] As already noted, when a Canadian connects to a server located in India to buy goods made in China from a company based in Luxembourg, the Canadian tax system cannot tax adequately the income arising from the transaction. In 2008, eBay paid only €33 tax in France while Amazon paid absolutely nothing![2]

E-commerce continues to grow in scope, bringing with it unprecedented problems for tax authorities, including difficulties in determining income and consumption taxes, as well as administrative problems in tax collection. In 2009, then-federal Revenue Minister Jean-Pierre Blackburn said that it was impossible to assess the tax losses that the Canadian government incurs in cyberspace. He noted, however, that "electronic transactions by Canadians have reached approximately US$5 billion per year."[3]

THE GROWING SCOPE OF E-COMMERCE

By the early 1990s the Internet had evolved to the point where, for the first time, it was being used as a virtual store. A decade later, thousands of companies in western Europe and the United States were advertising their products on the Web. By 2010, e-commerce was no longer a cutting-edge practice but a business necessity.

The potential for e-commerce development is enormous. According to research published in 2010 by the European Commission, more than 250 million Europeans use the Internet every day.[4] Canada's penetration rate of more than 80 per cent puts the country in twelfth place on the list of countries with the highest Internet usage.[5]

The United States is recognized as the pioneer of electronic commerce, and the industry continues to grow. In 2009, its revenues were estimated at $130 billion and they are expected to reach $223.9 billion in 2014. In 2010, 169 million U.S. Internet users shopped on the net, and more than 80 per cent of them made purchases. Amazon.com, for example, receives 615 million visits to its site annually.[6]

E-COMMERCE AND TAX: A COMPLEX RELATIONSHIP

The question of taxing transactions made through electronic commerce has been the subject of much thought and work, at both the national and the international level. Two opposing theories have emerged. Some believe that it's necessary to exempt e-commerce from taxes in order to promote its development. At the other end of the spectrum, others maintain that nontaxation of Internet sales could cost countries billions of dollars. In their view, taxing e-commerce is necessary to promote equality of economic opportunity in global trade and to prevent tax avoidance or evasion by Internet sellers.[7]

At the international level, basic principles for taxing electronic commerce were established at the OECD ministerial meeting in Ottawa in 1998. A compromise needed to be reached between countries that supported the principle of unconstrained development of electronic commerce and those that favoured new taxes. The OECD suggested that the general principles of taxation apply to electronic commerce and that electronic transactions be taxed as services and at the point of consumption.[8] This conservative approach did not preclude new administrative or legislative measures governing electronic commerce or changes in existing provisions, provided that such measures are intended to facilitate the application of existing taxation principles and do not seek to impose discriminatory taxes on e-commerce transactions. Since then, the OECD's work has proceeded on the basis of these principles. Several countries, including Canada, have pledged to follow the guidelines established by the OECD.[9]

The United States has adopted a hands-off policy in the face of the challenges posed by e-commerce. The Internet Tax Freedom Act, signed in 1998 by President Bill Clinton, aimed to promote and preserve the Internet's commercial, educational and information potential. This law prohibits federal, state and local governments from taxing the Internet by preventing taxes on items such as bandwidth or email and prohibits multiple taxes on electronic commerce. It has been extended three times by Congress since its enactment. The current moratorium is in force until November 1, 2014.

With the economic crisis, U.S. states are seeking tax resources, and there are proposals to tax online sales in a growing number of states. In North Carolina and California, for example, new tax regimes will take effect in 2012. New York state already taxes online sales.

In France, the "Google tax" has been the subject of

extensive discussion in 2011. In the end, this 1 per cent tax on the purchase of advertising space failed to make it through the National Assembly.[10] Its purpose was to capture some revenue from Internet giants established abroad for tax purposes, but the government was opposed because it would have affected French small- and medium-sized enterprises that wish to operate through the Internet, and not the big Internet players initially targeted.

CORPORATE TAX RULES ARE OBSOLETE

A business can serve multiple countries without having to establish sales offices. A website can be hosted anywhere and moved easily. Web servers move quickly from one country to another without having to change their domain name. Companies can link their domain name to a server located anywhere in the world.[11] Businesses are so mobile that tax authorities in Canada and other countries with high tax rates may lose their power to tax businesses with revenue that stems from electronic commerce.

Most countries, including Canada, use *residency status* or *source of income* to determine tax liability. Countries usually tax companies resident in their territory based on their world-wide income. Foreign companies are taxed only on income earned within the country, including commercial profits made by a permanent establishment located in the country and other amounts such as royalties, interest and dividends paid to foreign companies by the country's residents.

The residency of a corporation is generally determined based on the "place of incorporation" or "place of central management and control." With the advent of the Internet, taxpayers can easily thwart these criteria. A company that engages in e-commerce can easily take up residence anywhere, including tax havens. Electronic communication tools such as videoconferencing make it extremely difficult to determine the place of central management and control of a company.

According to the traditional principle, a country may tax the profits made by a foreign company if the company has a permanent establishment on its territory. A permanent establishment is generally defined as a "fixed place of business where the business activities are exercised in whole or in part." The term *fixed* means attachment to a particular location for a specified minimum period of time. Since a website is not considered a permanent establishment, countries cannot tax the profits attributable to sales in the territory through a website. Servers and other computer technologies meet the physical demands, but only in some circumstances.[12]

Even if all countries agreed that a website constitutes a permanent establishment, loss of revenue would not stop for long. A company could avoid having a permanent establishment in a country by constantly moving its website from one server in one country to another server in another country, or could set up its website on a server in a tax haven. Given this complex situation, should the current definition of "permanent establishment" be revised, or should special tax arrangements be created to deal with electronic commerce? And which are preferable, tax rules based on the taxpayers' residence or those based on source of income?

RULES FOR CONSUMPTION TAXES ARE INADEQUATE

In most countries, consumption taxes are applicable irrespective of whether the property is tangible or intangible or whether the seller is established in the country or not. The general principle is that a particular good or service is taxed according to where it is consumed. While this principle works well for traditional trade, it does not for e-commerce.

For example, when downloading music from a foreign site, consumers are able to escape these taxes. The same scenario occurs when people download computer programs, games, books, newspapers, magazines and the like. The problem comes from the fact that there are no customs in the virtual world. As an alternative, it is expected that the consumer must self-report—an obligation that is purely theoretical and rarely observed in reality.

Unfair competition therefore takes place between traditional and online merchants, and this is reflected in lower tax revenues. In April 2009, the newspaper *Métro* reported that nearly half of online purchases by Quebecers were made from American businesses, leading to a loss of more than $100 million to the province's economy.[13] This unfair competition also results in fewer direct and indirect jobs, since e-commerce companies require less labour than traditional commerce. Between April 2007 and April 2008, eBay Canada had only seven employees across the country and still pocketed US$1 billion.[14]

THE DIFFICULTIES OF TAX ADMINISTRATION

The Internet was developed by the U.S. military during the Cold War to transmit information securely in the event of an enemy attack. The unpredictable path of information technology now allows its users to enjoy relative anonymity in their electronic transactions, resulting in tracking problems for the IRS.[15] There is not yet a sufficiently effective means to track taxpayers and taxable transactions concluded via the Internet. Taxpayers can have several email addresses and act under false identities—but that may not be the most serious problem. Mukesh Arya, an expert on auditing in the virtual world, fears that multinationals are developing strategies for tax evasion by listing a false place of origin for their transactions.[16]

The case *eBay Canada Ltd.* v. *Minister of National Revenue*[17] illustrates the tracking difficulties that tax authorities may encounter. The legal battle lasted more than two years and ended up in the Federal Court of Appeal.[18] As part of an investigation to determine whether Canadians who sold goods through eBay reported their income, the CRA asked eBay Canada to provide certain information regarding its users, such as names, addresses, telephone numbers and sales figures. When the company refused to cooperate, the CRA obtained a court order forcing it to supply the information. Following that, eBay Canada asked the Federal Court to set aside the order.

The Federal Court ruled in favour of the CRA. It interpreted the law so that a resident of Canada can be required to provide information to which he or she has access for commercial purposes in Canada, even if that information is stored in databases owned by a third party outside Canada. The Court stated that "such information cannot truly be said to 'reside' only in one place or be 'owned' by only one person. The reality is that the information is readily and instantaneously available to those within the group of eBay entities in a variety of places." In the same vein, the Court of Appeals judge said it would be extremely formalistic to conclude that the information was not located in Canada before it was downloaded to a computer located in Canada.[19] He was of the opinion that the information was located in Canada because eBay Canada could easily access and use it as part of its business within Canada.[20]

Eric Schmidt, executive chairman of Google, said that the right to privacy needed to be redefined. In his view, nations will have no choice but to favour the public good and higher tax revenues over respect for the anonymity of Internet users.[21] In the *eBay* case, the court noted that in a tax system based on self-assessment, privacy expectations in regard to business records are very low. An obligation to provide information is the least intrusive way for the minister to ensure taxpayers' compliance in submitting their returns.[22]

If the right to privacy weakens, one of the solutions to these tax administration problems could be to trace taxpayers by their IP addresses. After all, the police already use this method to combat child pornography, for example. Furthermore, any expectation of absolute privacy on the Internet may be waning, if it ever was strong. Many Internet users freely divulge details of their personal lives on social networks, or have them divulged by their social network "friends." And it is generally known that Internet user data is not fully private and secure (try Googling "the Internet is not secure"). It would seem odd to insist on a bubble of absolute privacy and security in the case of taxation of Internet transactions.

It is difficult to predict what the future holds for the taxation of electronic commerce. Until a consensus can be reached at the international level, tax authorities in individual nation-states must hope they can succeed in managing the growing negative consequences of nontaxation of the Web.

5

PRIVATE FOUNDATIONS (AKA CHARITY FOR THE RICH)

The number of private charitable foundations has been increasing exponentially in North America. At the time the Rockefeller Foundation was created in 1913,[1] there were only a few private foundations in the United States. There were 70,480 in 1998, and more than 120,000 in 2011.[2] In Canada, as of December 2010, there were 4,937 private charitable foundations with total assets of $19.4 billion.[3]

Charity is important. In his 2006 encyclical *Deus Caritas Est* ("God is love"), Pope Benedict XVI praised the many organizations devoted to charitable or philanthropic purposes. However, the tax system needs to have an honest approach to charity—unlike the approach it has now to private foundations. The tax rules related directly and incidentally to private foundations are not fair to taxpayers in general and are legally too lax.

Basically, here's how the rules work. First, there are millionaires and billionaires who receive overly generous tax exemptions because they transfer the wealth they would never be able to spend in their lifetimes to their private foundations, over which they retain full control. In exchange, the rules should obligate the foundations to spend this wealth for charitable purposes that benefit society, but this is not the case. The only amount a foundation has to spend for charitable purposes is the return on this wealth. This enables the foundation to perpetuate itself while protecting the initial capital. Sooner or later, taxpayers are bound to react to this system.

THE WORLD'S MAJOR PRIVATE CHARITABLE FOUNDATIONS

The Canadian-based MasterCard Foundation, established in 2006 by MasterCard Worldwide, is funded though the donation of just over 15 per cent of the company's shares. This foundation supports activities designed to fight world poverty, such as microfinance and youth education.[4] It has $3 billion in assets.

The Lucie and André Chagnon Foundation is another Canadian foundation, established after the sale of Vidéotron to Quebecor Media in 2000. André Chagnon transferred $1.4 billion to the foundation, whose mission is "to contribute to the development and improvement of health through the prevention of poverty and disease, by focusing primarily on children and their parents." The foundation had assets of $1,333,976,000 and fifty-four full-time employees as of December 31, 2010. Its annual budget is currently $87,184,000.

The largest foundation in the United States is the Bill and Melinda Gates Foundation, with assets of $36 billion. The size of its operations far exceeds the level of humanitarian aid that many countries can provide, and its operating budget for health issues is equal to that of the World Health Organization. At the G8 summit held in Huntsville, Ontario, in June 2010, at which major maternal health programs were launched, the Gates Foundation signed a cheque for US$1.5 billion to fund them, a sum greater than the C$1.4 billion given by Canada.[5]

Since the Bill and Melinda Gates Foundation was established in 2000,[6] it has spent US$25 billion to improve access to education and health in the United States and in poor countries. In 2011, the foundation employed 950 people. It donated on the order of $2.6 billion in 2010.[7]

The INGKA Foundation in Sweden, valued at $36 billion, is the world's largest in terms of assets, but its founder, Ingvar Kamprad, has a reputation for stinginess. Founded in 1982, the INGKA Foundation holds all the shares of INGKA Holding, a company established in the Netherlands that owns 207 of the 235 IKEA stores worldwide. While the foundation's mission is to encourage innovation in architecture and interior design, it is not very active and has made only a few donations since its inception. For example, it granted $1.7 million to the Lund Institute of Technology in Sweden for 2004 and 2005.[8]

The list of private foundations is long, and they are scattered all over the planet. They include the Ford Foundation, the Wellcome Trust and many more.[9] The popularity of foundations will likely grow in the coming decades. In the summer of 2010, Warren Buffett and Bill Gates launched the Giving Pledge campaign, whose objective is to encourage America's 403 billionaires to offer some of their wealth to philanthropic organizations. By August 2011, sixty-nine billionaires had pledged. Knowing that the 400 richest Americans together have $1.2 trillion, Gates and Buffett hope to raise about $600 billion—nearly three times Canada's annual budget. The billionaires who have already joined the Giving Pledge campaign include New York City Mayor Michael Bloomberg, media owner Ted Turner, Oracle cofounder Larry Ellison, former Cisco Systems president John Morgridge and Microsoft cofounder Paul Allen.[10]

THE LAWS GOVERNING PRIVATE FOUNDATIONS

In Canada, as in most other countries, governments encourage the private practice of charity and philanthropy through tax incentives. Tax measures that favour charitable giving have evolved over the last century. Today, Canadian taxpayers may deduct close to 50 per cent (29 per cent federally and 24 per cent in Quebec due to the refundable Quebec abatement) of the amount of donations made to charities from the tax they owe the government. Donations of certain publicly traded securities (such as shares, bonds and mutual funds) are even more advantageous because they are exempt from taxation on capital gains, normally applicable at the point of sale.

There are three types of charitable organizations: public foundations, private foundations and charities. Charities are distinguished from the others by their active orientation. Generally, charities must devote all their resources to the charitable activities that they conduct themselves. Foundations fund charitable activities conducted by other organizations.

The difference between public foundations and private foundations lies in the nature of their control. A private foundation is controlled by a single donor or one family through a board of directors at least 50 per cent of whom are tied to the donor or the family. In contrast, a public foundation is governed by a board composed of a majority of unrelated directors and usually receives its funding from multiple donors with no links between them.

"Registered" charities enjoy two privileges: they do not pay taxes, and they can issue official receipts that allow donors to receive tax credits.

To be "registered" by the Canada Revenue Agency, charities must work towards specific goals that the courts have recognized as charitable, such as poverty relief, the advancement of education or religion or other purposes that benefit the entire community.

The rules that charities must follow are found primarily in the tax code. They regulate the investments, business activities, political activities, loans, grants and international activities that charities can carry out. In addition, charities must comply with a "disbursement quota" under which they must spend a minimum amount annually for charitable purposes. We look at the deficiencies of these rules in the next section; a fuller description of the rules can be found in Appendix 3.

THE FIVE KEY SHORTCOMINGS OF PRIVATE FOUNDATIONS

Private foundations pose a wide variety of problems to all of us. Let's start with Problem Number 1: The threat to democracy. As Abraham Lincoln said, democracy is "government of the people, by the people, for the people." The current rules governing private foundations bypass the political system because they allow founders to appropriate a piece of public power, which in a democracy should be granted only to the people or individuals whom voters have elected. As things stand, private foundations may be on the way to becoming a new world order.

As early as 1789, Thomas Jefferson, later the third president of the United States, identified the problem: "Private fortunes should be dissolved by the abolition of the law of primogeniture and of their unalienable character. Otherwise, a few individuals and institutions could raise with time enough wealth to govern ordinary citizens." In 1915, two years after the creation of the Rockefeller Foundation, the U.S. Congress felt the need to investigate the activities of large foundations. The commission established for this purpose concluded,

> *The domination by the men in whose hands the*
> *final control of a large part of American industry*
> *rests is not limited to their employees, but is*
> *rapidly being extended to control the education*
> *and social survival of the nation. This control is*
> *being extended largely through the creation of*
> *enormous privately managed funds for indefinite*
> *purposes, hereafter designated "foundations."*[11]

In the early 1950s, the U.S. Congress once again became interested in the activities of private foundations. The Reece Committee concluded that the power granted to private foundations posed a threat to democratic government. The committee noted that some of the largest foundations had actively supported attacks on the social and governmental system of the United States and had financed the promotion of socialism and collectivist ideas. The committee proposed that the law be amended to impose a time limit on each foundation's existence.[12]

It also appears that the people who run and administer private foundations do not reflect the racial and cultural diversity of the communities they serve.[13] In 2006, a survey of 802 private foundations revealed that only 23.2 per cent of employees and 13 per cent of directors in the United States belonged to a racial group other than white, compared to the national average of 33.8 per cent.[14]

Apart from the obligation to provide grants to recipients that meet qualifications set by tax authorities, foundations have total freedom to choose in which projects they will invest in. This arrangement can therefore help one group of recipient organizations at the expense of others. According to that same study of 802 private foundations conducted in 2006, only 7.4 per cent of total grant dollars were distributed to minority/ethnic communities.[15]

Here's Problem Number 2 with private foundations. According to Canadian tax laws, private foundations must spend a minimum amount each year on charitable activities. The percentage required is called the disbursement quota, and since March 2010 the disbursement quota for private foundations has been set at 3.5 per cent. So every year, private charitable foundations must spend on charitable activities, or give to qualified recipients, an amount equal to or greater than 3.5 per cent of their capital.[16]

There was a time in Canada when the disbursement quota payment imposed on charitable foundations was substantially higher.[17] The reduction in the disbursement quota allows Canadian foundations to keep their startup capital. The founders can then rest assured that their foundations will last indefinitely. They argue that the charitable impact will be greater in the long term if private foundations preserve their capital and distribute only the returns. But not everyone agrees with this way of thinking, especially in recessionary times.

Some feel that foundations established to meet genuine priorities of today will not necessarily meet the needs of future generations. In an article published in the *New York Times* in 2008, Ray D. Madoff referred to the case of Leona Helmsley, the wealthy American who left $8 billion in a perpetual foundation for the maintenance and welfare of dogs. He concluded, "If this were only a matter of Leona Helmsley wasting her own money, no one would need to care. But she is wasting ours too."[18] He added,

> By setting aside assets for the uncertain needs
> of the future, we deprive ourselves of resources
> for addressing the obvious and compelling needs
> of today. The idea is that the world has many

pressing problems, and if we can focus resources on them today, through an investment approach, we will minimize the need for dealing with them more urgently and less thoughtfully as crises later on.

Trustees sometimes have the power to change a foundation's objectives, but there is no obligation to do so, and donors receive tax benefits irrespective of whether the foundation is meeting current needs. Besides, is it really necessary to keep capital for the future? After all, new billionaires and their foundations will arise and new wealth will enter the philanthropic stage, so it is not necessary to preserve the initial capital in perpetuity.

Several major philanthropists oppose the idea that foundations should be perpetual, arguing that wealth should be spent during the person's lifetime. Julius Rosenwald, who established the Julius Rosenwald Fund in 1917, wrote,

I am not in sympathy with...perpetuating endowment and believe that more good can be accomplished by expending funds as trustees find opportunities for constructive work than by storing a large sum of money for long periods of time. By adopting the policy of using the fund within this generation, we may avoid these tendencies toward bureaucracy and a formal or perfunctory attitude toward the work which almost invariably develops in organisations which prolong their existences indefinitely. Coming generations can be relied upon to provide for their own needs as they arise.

Chuck Feeney, a billionaire Irish-American philanthropist, argues that people should give while they are alive. His philosophy is largely influenced by Andrew Carnegie's "Gospel of Wealth," which expressed the view "that people of substantial wealth potentially create problems for future generations unless they themselves accept responsibility to use their wealth during their lifetime to help worthwhile causes." In his book *Inside American Philanthropy*, Waldemar Nielsen writes, "Time is not the friend of foundation vigor and effectiveness. In fact, with the passing of years, decay and stagnation are quite common, if not endemic."

The permanence of foundations also calls into question the nature of the original gift. When a founder creates a private foundation and transfers his or her wealth into it, is it logical that the founder should receive a tax receipt for the amount transferred to the foundation, considering that, ultimately, this capital is rarely spent for charitable purposes? For example, if Mr. X, a Canadian resident, donates $100 million to his foundation in 2012, which will not be spent for charitable purposes, is it logical for the tax system to grant him a saving of $50 million? In this example, the founder enjoys a tax saving of about $50 million in year one, and only $3.5 million has to be invested by the private foundation for charitable purposes in society each year. Thus, it could take more than twenty years to replenish the public coffers.

Finally, it is puzzling that the transfer should qualify as a gift for legal purposes. A gift implies that the donor divests himself or herself irrevocably of the property in question in favour of another person, without compensation and with a generous spirit. Canadian federal and provincial tax laws contain several specific anti-avoidance rules that prevent taxpayers from accruing a tax advantage by simulating gifts to themselves or related persons.

What's Problem Number 3? Under the current regime, the founder generally becomes CEO of the foundation, which usually carries his or her name. Thus, regardless of skills, that person becomes the guiding hand for the funds accumulated by the organization, financed in large part by taxpayer dollars.

Those who defend philanthrocapitalism believe that it is a great benefit to society to have the biggest capitalists put their talents and methods of working in the service of managing "social affairs."[19] Thus, Warren Buffett, in giving a significant part of his fortune to the Gates Foundation, expressed complete confidence in Bill and Melinda Gates's expertise. With Bill Gates and the rest of the world looking on, he explained at a press conference on the morning of the gift, "Whatever you want to do, what is more logical than to look for someone better equipped than you to do it?" and "Who wouldn't pick Tiger Woods to play in his place in a golf tournament?"

There are a number of caveats to be noted regarding the idea that large private entrepreneurs would naturally be competent to manage charitable foundations. First, they rarely have the time required; they generally need to choose between running the business or running the foundation. For example, Bill Gates decided as of 2008 to devote more energy to the foundation he had established eight years earlier than to his company, Microsoft.[20]

Nor is it always true that a person with a knack for generating profit in a business will have the same capacity for solving social problems and being involved in issues of public interest. For example, Sam Walton's ability to develop the largest chain of big-box stores in the world does not necessarily put him in the best position to know how best to redistribute money from his foundation to society at large. The opposite is also true and may be easier to see. The best president of the

United States would not necessarily be the best president of a multinational corporation. The necessary decisions in the two spheres, social and commercial, are made for completely different purposes and require different skills. Even within a company, leaders normally excel more at one stage of development than another. For example, those who are best at launching a startup are not always the best to run a company that has reached its cruising speed.

Problem Number 4 is that, in the world of charity—and especially in the world of private foundations—there appears to be more tolerance than elsewhere for serious misconduct and unreasonable expenses, and senior management faces no real accountability and does not fear competition.

In Africa, in 2009, between $215 and $360 million was wasted on water supply projects because the charities responsible had not planned for network maintenance. According to a report produced in 2010 by the International Institute for Environment and Development,[21] approximately 50,000 water supply points have disappeared because of this carelessness.

In the United States, the Center for Promise and Opportunity (CPO), a charity founded by John Edwards, a candidate for the 2008 Democratic presidential nomination, paid $124,000 in 2006 for videos and photos taken by Rielle Hunter. These videos and pictures were listed as one of the Center's activities, but they have never been seen. It also turned out that Edwards had an affair with Rielle Hunter in 2006. Patricia Fiori, counsel for CPO, defended the failure to provide the videos, explaining that CPO had terminated its activities and its website was not operational. She added that, in any case, it is common to hire people to write speeches that are never delivered![22]

Canadian tax authorities have access to a range of tools and sanctions to ensure that charities comply with the law. Most apply at the organizational level, but in some circumstances directors may be held personally liable. For example, directors may face personal liability if the company fails to comply with legal requirements relating to the company's activities, the duty to report, the allocation of funds and the issuance of receipts for gifts. They can also be held accountable if the organization fails to collect and remit GST, HST or Quebec sales tax.[23] In court, some judges have imposed higher obligations on directors of charities than on those of for-profit companies, precisely because of the privileges enjoyed by those organizations.[24]

In practice, however, the harshest penalty generally applied at the organizational level is revocation of the charity's privileged tax status. This is true even though authorities have had the power since 2004 to impose intermediate sanctions that would result in financial penalties. The Auditor General of Canada's report released in the fall of 2010 noted that the CRA does not have sufficiently detailed internal guidance to support the application of sanctions.[25] The report revealed that between April 2006 and March 2009 the CRA continued to use letters of awareness, compliance agreements and revocation of charitable status to enforce the law, while it rarely imposed intermediate sanctions. In fact, there were 127 revocations for cause and only two sanctions other than revocation.

Unlike businesses and elected officials, charitable foundations therefore operate in an environment where accountability is negligible. This freedom given to foundations may seem in harmony with the principles of capitalist management, but the reality is quite different. The other key element essential to the capitalist model is lacking in this situation—competition, to rein in the freedom to act. In the current legislative context, foundations, and especially large, financially strong ones, are immune from any form of competition.

The current system does not encourage charities to carry out high-quality activities. The Canada Revenue Agency ensures that charitable foundations have goals consistent with the definition of "charitable," but it has no way of knowing whether donations are being used strategically and efficiently. Substantial amounts are lost each year because, unlike firms in which profit targets inform management procedures, private foundations are not aiming at profitability. Another kind of incentive is needed to keep them efficient.

The fifth problem with private foundations is that the CRA does not exercise tight enough supervision and is not transparent in carrying out its duties related to charities.

The Canada Revenue Agency has approximately 41,000 employees.[26] Of those employees, 270 work for the Charities Directorate at headquarters in Ottawa, and there are also forty field auditors who carry out charity audits across Canada.[27] Thus, Canada's 85,000 charitable organizations, issuing tax receipts worth $13.9 billion annually, are monitored by only forty field auditors.[28]

According to the OECD's 2009 *Report on Abuse of Charities for Money-Laundering and Tax Evasion*, based on information provided to the organization by nineteen countries in 2008, Canada could expect to lose $200 million annually in taxes through fraud linked to the charitable sector.[29] In Canada there are several techniques for scamming the system or the donors.

One such technique is for an organization pretending to be registered with the CRA to solicit funds from the public (by telephone, by mail or door-to-door) for a particular cause and issue false tax receipts.[30] Between 2002 and 2006, the CanAfrica International Foundation issued false donation receipts for an estimated $38 million. Ambrose Danso-Dapaah, president of the Toronto-based foundation, pleaded guilty to fraud and was sentenced to fifty-one months in prison.

In other cases, an organization appropriately approved by the CRA seeks public funds which its directors then use for personal purposes.[31] The Wish Kids Foundation, located in Woodstock, Ontario, had amassed $900,000. Instead of using the money to help terminally ill children to fulfill their dreams as the foundation proclaimed, the president bought a vehicle, paid for flying lessons for his son and made a deposit towards the purchase of an airplane.[32] The leaders of the Universal Aide Society, located in Nanaimo, British Columbia, whose proclaimed mission is to help people in need around the world, used donations it received to travel between their homes in Vancouver, British Columbia, and Nice, France, buy icewine and cigarettes and pay unjustified fees to employees, directors and family members.[33]

Still another possibility: a registered organization sells its tax receipts.[34] Between 2003 and 2009, charitable tax shelters involved 161,500 taxpayers and $5.15 billion in donations. Using a range of methods, each more complex than the last, the organizations provide donors with receipts for amounts of up to five times the actual amount of their donation or more (for example, a tax receipt for $10,000 can sell for $1,000 or $2,000).

Given the CRA's lack of transparency in performing its audit work and its limited resources for reaching the general public, it is very difficult for a taxpayer to ensure that a charity is in good standing and really does charitable work. Indeed, the CRA reveals the results of an audit only when a registered charity's status is revoked. If an auditor discovers that an organization does not do what it claims to do, but the finding does not lead to revocation of its status, tax rules prohibit the CRA from notifying taxpayers. Donors can visit the government's online database to check the financial condition of charities registered in Canada, but the CRA does not guarantee the validity of the information.

Finally, it should be mentioned that at its 2011 annual conference,[35] the Council on Foundations, an organization of American foundations that provides services and support to its members, put philanthropy "on trial."[36] The question was whether private foundations fulfill their mission to serve the public good.

The prosecution painted a damning picture of philanthropy and criticized the tax benefits available to private foundations. It said that while we've come to expect lobbyists to argue for tax breaks for their clients, the American people have real needs such as guaranteed health care and no more tax breaks for the rich. For its part, the defence described the importance of philanthropy and the charitable sector. It argued that even if it is not perfect, the sector continues to pursue the common good.

In the end, ten of twelve jurors found the accused guilty!

6

GREENING THE TAX SYSTEM

G reen taxation means altering the prices of goods and
services as a way of inducing people and corporations to behave in environmentally positive ways,
or deterring them from behaving in environmentally negative ways.[1] It can involve a number of taxes, user fees and tax
incentives (the various fiscal tools are described more fully
in Appendix 3). It can also be a more comprehensive change:
Environmental Fiscal Reform (EFR) is a term that can be
used to describe a program aimed at bringing environmental
value into the very foundation of a tax system. An EFR system
taxes (and thus deters) pollution while cutting taxes on (and
thus encouraging) labour or other desired values. It provides
a coherent frame of reference, setting it apart from piecemeal
tax measures. The revenues it pulls in can be used to finance
environmental protection measures, bring down the debt,
increase public investment or reduce individual and corporate income taxes. EFR is seen as paying a "double dividend,"
promoting both environmentally respectful conduct and
economic recovery.

A number of countries have shifted or are shifting to

green taxation, among them Germany, Denmark and Britain. The Australian government of Prime Minister Julia Gillard indicated in 2011 that it intended to institute a carbon tax. Legislation had been passed to impose a tax on greenhouse gas emissions by the country's 500 largest polluters with the aim of reducing pollution, altering energy use and promoting investment in clean energy. This tax was to take effect by July 2012.[2]

In Canada, the idea of putting green taxes to greater use is not entirely new. The National Round Table on the Environment and the Economy (NRTEE)[3] made a set of proposals to this effect in 2002. In its 2005 budget, the government announced that it intended to consult Canadians about how the tax system could be put to better use in meeting environmental goals.[4] Since then, apart from an EFR plank in Liberal leader Stéphane Dion's 2008 election platform, there has been no major push in Canada at the federal level to implement green taxation.

Green taxation is a smart solution. It lets the market balance costs and benefits in the transfer of financial resources from polluting activities to cleaner endeavours. But implementing it runs up against major political challenges. Philippe Faucher of the Université de Montréal points out that because the costs are concentrated among the major polluters, while the benefits are so widely diluted, there is a significant political challenge to adopting a carbon tax.[5]

CANADA'S MAIN ENVIRONMENTAL TAXES

A list of Canada's existing green tax measures shows that this area of taxation is not highly developed in comparison with most other industrialized countries.[6]

Table 1

Tax	Amount
Excise tax on gasoline	10 cents per litre
Excise tax on vehicle air conditioners	$100 per air conditioner
Excise tax on fuel-inefficient vehicles	At least 13 but less than 14 litres per 100 kilometres: $1,000 At least 14 but less than 15 litres per 100 kilometres: $2,000 At least 15 but less than 16 litres per 100 kilometres: $3,000 16 litres or more per 100 kilometres: $4,000

Source: OECD

Figure 1 shows environmental tax revenues as a percentage of GDP in all OECD countries. In 2009, this ratio was 1.2 per cent for Canada, lower than any other country except Chile, New Zealand, the United States and Mexico.

Figure 1: Revenues from environmentally related taxes as a percentage of GDP, OECD countries

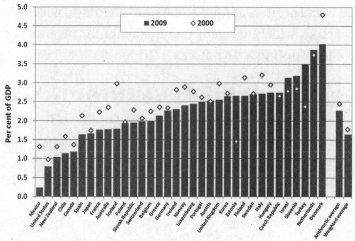

Source: OECD, *More information on environmentally related taxes, fees and charges*, retrieved from
www2.oecd.org/ecoinst/queries/Taxinfo.htm

In Canada, federal green taxes consist almost entirely of fuel taxes. In addition, there is a $100 excise tax on air condition-ers in new vehicles and an excise tax on gas-guzzling vehicles. The federal excise tax on diesel fuel is set at four cents a litre. In 2008, the Conservative election platform called for it to be lowered to two cents, though it has not been changed. Some provinces also apply taxes on diesel fuel: Alberta (nine cents a litre), British Columbia (eight to fourteen cents), Ontario (fourteen cents) and Quebec (sixteen cents). In addition to fuel taxes, the main provincial and municipal green taxes are carbon taxes in British Columbia and Quebec and Ontario's Tax for Fuel Conservation, imposed on the purchase of the most fuel-inefficient vehicles. The provinces have also adopted and are planning an array of environmental fees: fees for recycling electronic equipment, tires and paint, as well as deposits on containers, fees for the disposal or recycling of packaging, fees for hunting permits and the like.

WHY ISN'T THE CANADIAN TAX SYSTEM GREENER?

Green taxation in Canada faces a number of challenges. The main ones are: the desire among some for Canada to harmonize its policy with the United States; the major interregional wealth transfers it could produce; Canada's economic reliance on the oil industry; constitutional issues; and insufficient environmental consciousness among Canadian voters. Each of these five obstacles is described more fully in the following pages.

Let's start with Canada's perceived need to harmonize policy with the United States.

Canada has historically taken a subordinate approach towards the United States. When George W. Bush was U.S. president, Stephen Harper decided to reject the tough targets set under the Kyoto Protocol, even though his Liberal predecessor had ratified this agreement in 2005. Harper then agreed to promote North American energy integration, and Canada remained a reliable hydrocarbon supplier to the United States. Canadians have often chided Harper for stating in 2002 that "Kyoto is essentially a socialist scheme" designed to suck money out of rich countries.[7] But he later claimed it was President Bush's inaction in environmental matters that prevented Canada from taking more radical measures against climate change.[8] In 2007, Canada joined the Asia-Pacific Partnership on Clean Development and Climate, a Bush administration initiative. This nonbinding international agreement, parallel to the Kyoto Protocol, was signed by Australia, China, India, Japan, South Korea and the United States. The partnership aimed "to accelerate the development, deployment and diffusion of cleaner, more efficient technologies as a way to reduce air pollution, secure a sustainable supply of energy and to mitigate climate change."[9]

After the election of Barack Obama as president, Canada emphasized its intention to emulate U.S. climate change policy in all respects.[10] President Obama tried to persuade Congress to adopt a wide-ranging energy and climate bill aimed at reducing greenhouse gas emissions. There were hopes for a new dialogue between Canada and the United States. However, despite intense negotiations, Democratic senators failed to convince their colleagues of the importance of taking action. Democratic Majority Leader Harry Reid announced the end of talks on July 22, 2010. This meant an indefinite postponement in establishing a U.S. carbon tax or cap-and-trade system. Republican victories in midterm elections later that year further solidified this postponement.

Choosing how to follow up on the Kyoto Protocol, which was set to expire in 2012, was the central issue at a summit planned for Durban, South Africa, in December 2011.

Forecasts were not optimistic. Japan, Russia and Canada had already let it be known that they would not sign on to an additional period if the United States and the larger emerging countries such as China (expected to be the world's biggest greenhouse gas emitter in 2012) also refused to enter into the agreement—a predictable outcome.[11] After participating in the summit, Canada withdrew from the Kyoto Protocol.

Although negotiations had hit a dead end, not all was lost. Whether or not there was a post-Kyoto agreement, Canada and the United States could be forced to make a green shift. Even if China did not agree to join in, all indications were that it would soon be taking serious action on climate change.

Climate change is a central priority in China. Aware that nonrenewable resources are inexorably running out, the country is already attempting to limit its energy dependency by turning to solar and wind energy and biofuels. International media are filled with news about the enormous investments the country is making in renewable energy and its efforts to save energy. According to a study by the Pew Charitable Trusts, Chinese investment in renewable energy and other "green" projects appears to have risen 39 per cent in 2010 over 2009, after many years of significant growth. In 2011, China agreed to reduce its energy intensity by 16 per cent over the next five years. In March 2011, Premier Wen Jiabao stated that seeking to slow economic growth to 7 per cent annually from an average of 10.6 per cent since 2006 would be "an opportunity to adjust the form of economic development and to deal with imbalances, lack of coordination and sustainability."[12]

The more China and other countries move towards a green shift, the more the United States and Canada will be forced to do the same. It should not be forgotten that China is a major economic partner of the United States and Canada and that it is second in GDP only to the United States among world economic powers[13] and is expected to overtake the United States within a decade.[14] Its strong economic growth and rising trade have given it a more influential role in the world economic system and boosted its political weight substantially. In his first official overseas visit in China in July 2011, Canadian Foreign Minister John Baird said, "Strengthening ties with China, which is home to one of the world's most important and fastest-growing economies, makes sense."[15] Canadian exports to China rose to $13.2 billion in 2010, up 18.7 per cent from a year earlier, and the country is now Canada's second biggest trading partner.

In theory, the adoption of a carbon tax should put the companies, industries, markets, organizations and administrations that are subject to it at an economic advantage if their greenhouse gas emissions are lower than those of their competitors. Adopting this type of tax may therefore lead to significant wealth transfers.

For a better understanding of these wealth transfers, consider the following example. Let us suppose that a government adopts a policy under which households receive one free garbage bag per week and unused bags can be sold to other households at a price set by the government. Under this policy, households that produce less than one bagful of garbage a week obviously come out ahead. The losers are those who can't adjust their way of life to this new policy and who, accordingly, produce more than one bagful of garbage per week.

The garbage bag analogy illustrates the wealth transfer that can occur between groups when the ecological cost of their conduct is embodied in markets. Individuals, families, industries, provinces, countries or continents that are bigger polluters risk becoming poorer. They need time to change their polluting habits.

Since the price of a tonne of greenhouse gas would likely rise sharply,[16] the economic advantages of implementing a carbon tax would increase substantially over time. But Canada would risk being hit by an intense period of destabilization caused by wealth transfers between regions and markets with disparate environmental profiles. That could lead to a "new economic and political order" in Canada (to paraphrase George W. Bush). How could the public finances of Alberta and Saskatchewan be rebalanced after a monetary value was attached to their environmental deficit? How would supporters of Quebec independence react to the extra wealth Quebec's ecological performance would bring their way? How could British Columbia reverse the growth in greenhouse gas emissions it was experiencing (up 27.5 per cent in 2006 compared to 1990)? Could attaching a value to greenhouse gas emissions cause a further shakeup in Ontario, already hurt by a decline in its manufacturing sector? For the first time in its history, the province began receiving equalization payments ($347 million in the 2009–10 fiscal year and nearly $1 billion for 2010–11).

Table 2 shows the disparities between the provinces in greenhouse gas emissions and gives a better idea of the issues involved in wealth transfers between regions. If we apply a value of $50 per tonne of greenhouse gas and assume emission levels equal to those in 2007 (see Table 2), taxing greenhouse gas emissions would impoverish each Albertan by an amount that could reach $3,500, with the Alberta economy taking a $12.3 billion hit[17] before redistributive measures are taken into account. By contrast, each Quebecer would be impoverished by $555. The result would thus be a transfer of wealth. Alberta and Saskatchewan would become less alluring to investors while the other provinces would become more attractive.

Table 2: Greenhouse gas emission profile, Canada and provinces, 2007

Quantity of green house gases emitted	Tonnes per capita	Total (megatonnes)
Canada	22.6	747.0*
Alberta	70.7	245.7
British Columbia	14.4	63.1
Manitoba	18.0	21.3
New Brunswick	24.9	18.7
Newfoundland & Labrador	20.8	10.5
Nova Scotia	22.1	20.6
Ontario	15.4	197.4
Prince Edward Island	15.1	2.1
Quebec	11.1	85.7
Saskatchewan	72.2	72.0
Territories**	21.4	2.2

* Provincial and territorial totals do not add up to the total for Canada as a result of rounding.
** Yukon, Northwest Territories and Nunavut

Source: Environment Canada, *National Inventory Report 1990–2007: Greenhouse Gas Sources and Sinks in Canada* (Ottawa, April 2009), retrieved from www.ec.gc.ca/Publications/ B77E6264-D0E3-45B5-BE56-5A395C0B7653%5CNationalInventoryReport19902007Greenhou seGasSourcesAndSinksInCanada.pdf

Table 3 shows the contribution of various industries to greenhouse gas emissions. Adopting a carbon tax can be expected to accentuate wealth transfers between different production sectors. Because of the disparities between the emission volumes of various industries,[18] conditions will shift to the advantage of some and to the disadvantage of others. For example, aluminum production would be favoured in comparison to steel production.

Table 3: Greenhouse gas emissions in Canada, selected sectors, 2008

Sector	Emissions in megatonnes of CO_2 equivalent
Fossil fuel production & refining	68
Mining & oil & gas extraction*	97
Electricity & heat generation	119
Domestic aviation	8.5
Agriculture	62
Railways	7
Aluminum production	7.4
Heavy-duty diesel vehicle transport	39.4

* Includes emissions from pipelines and fugitive sources.

Source: Environment Canada, *National Inventory Report 1990–2008: Part 1: Greenhouse Gas Sources and Sinks in Canada* (Ottawa, 2010), p. 21, retrieved from www.ec.gc.ca/publications/492D914C-2EAB-47AB-A045-C62B2CDACC29/

If taking the green shift requires Canadian companies to obtain a more ecological alternative product sourced in Canada, the overall economy will feel no ill effects. On the other hand, if Canadian companies need to source alternative products abroad, Canadian producers will be penalized on both domestic and export markets. The result will be wealth moving outside the country. The effect could vary, depending on the countries of origin of competing products.

Our economic dependency on the oil industry is a third challenge to greening the tax system. The Canadian sector most concerned by a green shift is, of course, the tar sands industry. Alberta's tar sands deposits are among the world's largest sources of oil.[19] Developing this resource poses major technical, economic and environmental problems.

According to Environment Canada, "the oil and gas

industry contributed almost 40 per cent of Canada's total emission increase between 1990 and 2008."[20] The tar sands alone accounted for 5 per cent of Canada's total emissions in 2008 (37 out of 734 megatonnes). Emissions from the tar sands have risen 120 per cent since 1990, from 16.8 to 37.7 megatonnes per year, even though the industry managed during this time to reduce emissions per barrel of oil produced by 39 per cent (a trend that has recently reversed).[21] A Conference Board study published in 2010, *Getting the Balance Right: The Oil Sands, Exporting and Sustainability*,[22] explains that we can expect total emissions to rise as production increases, doubling by 2015.

The tar sands are of major economic and political significance in Canada. According to the Alberta government, tar sands investments totalled $102 billion from 2000 to 2009, and additional investments of $140 billion were expected by the end of 2012.[23] Statistics Canada estimated that the oil and gas extraction industry contributed $39 billion to Canada's wealth in 2009, yet other sectors are much more important; this amounted only to about 3.2 per cent of the country's GDP that year.[24] Tar sands exploitation creates numerous jobs in Alberta and other Canadian provinces. A report published in July 2009 by the Canadian Energy Research Institute (CERI) says the tar sands lead to employment for 112,000 people across Canada— many, but still less than 1 per cent of Canada's 16 million jobs. This figure is expected to grow to more than 500,000 in the next twenty-five years, and many of those jobs will be created in provinces other than Alberta.[25]

Promoted as a means of facilitating Canadian tar sands exports, the Keystone XL pipeline project has been highly controversial, especially because of its environmental implications, and has attracted numerous protests by citizens and environmental groups.[26] The pipeline, which its developer

TransCanada Corporation said would cost US$13 billion, would be used to ship crude oil from the Alberta tar sands to Gulf of Mexico refineries, passing through the American heartland. It would stretch 2,700 kilometres from Hardisty, northeast of Calgary, crossing Montana, South Dakota, Nebraska and Kansas to reach a distribution hub in Oklahoma and refineries in Texas. The U.S. government rejected TransCanada's application in January 2012, at least for now.

In addition to supplying the United States, the oil industry in western Canada aims to serve demand from China. In August 2009, PetroChina International acquired 60 per cent of two Athabasca projects for $1.9 billion. In 2010, China Investment Corporation, a sovereign wealth fund, invested $1.2 billion in the Canadian oil and gas group Penn West Energy Trust, which claims significant reserves in northern Alberta. In April 2010, the Chinese oil group Sinopec purchased the 9.03 per cent share held by the U.S. firm ConocoPhillips in Syncrude, the largest tar sands operator, for $4.65 billion. Another firm, Kinder Morgan, owns and operates several pipelines in Canada, including the Trans Mountain Pipeline running from Edmonton to Vancouver. Ian Anderson, the president of Kinder Morgan Canada, stated in various forums in 2010 that "demand in Asia is clearly going to be an outlet for producers in Canada."[27] In 2011, Kinder Morgan Canada was negotiating the construction of a second pipeline aimed at meeting Asian demand. In addition, Enbridge Inc. operates a major pipeline network in Canada and the U.S. In 2010, this company was negotiating the building of the Northern Gateway Pipeline, intended to carry 525,000 barrels per day of Asia-bound oil from Edmonton to Kitimat, B.C.

Constitutional issues are yet another potential challenge to greening the tax system. When it comes to the environment broadly, Canadian constitutional law divides responsibilities between federal, provincial and municipal levels of government. As shown in Figure 2, environmental responsibility is dispersed: each level of government must do its share and act together with the others in trying to resolve problems. In relation to green taxation specifically, the constitutional division of powers is not optimally designed to allow for complete flexibility. Nevertheless, depending on the design of the measure, both the federal government and provincial governments have a number of relevant constitutional powers.

Voters are the last challenge to greening the tax system. Is the environmental consciousness of Canada voters what it should be?

Although Canadians sometimes say they favour green taxation, there is reason to doubt the depth of this commitment.[28] Canadians may well have a degree of ecological consciousness, but has it reached the level that could allow for a true green tax shift in Canada?

The importance of the environment in public opinion polling has varied over the years. The environment is generally seen as important, and during some periods it has been the top issue for Canadians. Health is another perennially important issue, as is the economy, especially in tough economic times. However, public opinion polling does not itself determine policy action; the government has acted on issues with far lower rankings in the polls, e.g. spending enormous sums on foreign wars and military buildups.

Polling in relation to carbon taxes similarly varies over time. In a poll conducted in May 2008 by McAllister Opinion Research for the Pembina Institute, 72 per cent of the Canadians questioned thought the new carbon tax adopted in British Columbia was "a step in the right direction."[29] A year later, a poll done by Harris/Decima for The Canadian Press,

Figure 2: Constitutional division of environmental responsibilities among levels of government

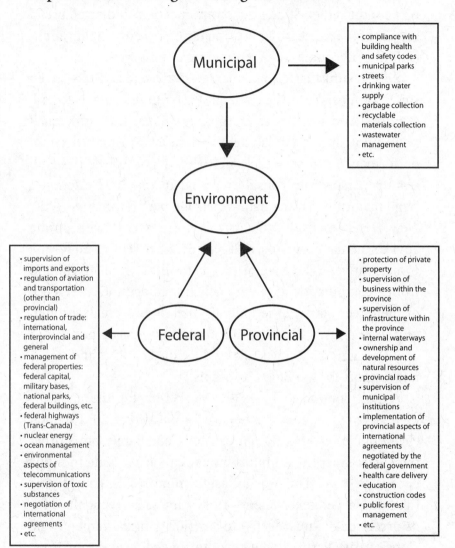

released on May 11, 2009, found that Canadians' positions had changed. Only 49 per cent agreed with adopting a tax on carbon emissions. And when asked if they would support a tax similar to the one adopted by British Columbia, which had the effect of increasing gasoline and fuel oil prices, only 42 per cent answered in the affirmative.[30] In the summer of 2011, a poll conducted by Strategic Communications indicated broad support for B.C.'s carbon tax, including broadening its application to all sources of greenhouse gas emissions.

Some claim that Canadians decisively rejected the "green shift" proposed by the Liberal Party in the 2008 federal election. And yet, things are not so simple. It is difficult, if not impossible, to attribute the Liberals' dismal electoral performance solely to the green shift plank of their overall platform, especially considering that in the 2008 election a large majority of Canadians voted for parties (including the New Democrats, Bloc Québécois and Greens) with strong environmental programs, and only 37.7 per cent voted for the Conservatives. The Liberal defeat resulted in all likelihood from a combination of factors which included the emergence of the Green Party,[31] the Liberals' inability to break through on the prairies,[32] a leader with limited popularity partly as a result of aggressive attack ads by the Conservatives and steadfast support for the Bloc Québécois.[33]

A poll conducted by Léger Marketing for the environmental group Équiterre a few weeks before the 2011 federal election showed that 70 per cent of Canadians claimed that the environment was important enough as an issue to influence their vote. This was an astonishing result, considering that the Harper government—not in any sense recognized for its green ideas—was elected to a majority in Parliament. The Conservative Party did not devote a single line to the environment in its seventy-five-page election platform.

Voters fear the potential regressive impact of green taxes. Green taxes can, depending on their design, be regressive, which means they could affect lower-income people more than others. This displeases, or may displease, a majority of voters. Carbon taxes primarily affect the price of energy consumption, and the poorest could be the most heavily penalized by a carbon tax. To get around this drawback, part of the proceeds from green taxes could be redistributed to low-income Canadians without endangering the hoped-for environmental benefits.

THINGS TO CONSIDER IN MOVING TOWARDS A SOLUTION

To overcome the challenges associated with implementation of green taxation in Canada, a number of elements need to be brought together: addressing the potential for wealth transfers between Canadian regions and between Canadian production sectors; optimizing the design of green tax measures; instituting incentives; and demonstrating the advantages of green taxation to voters whose main priority is often the economy.

On January 30, 2010, Jim Prentice, then the federal environment minister, committed Canada to a post-Kyoto target for 2020 that would bring greenhouse gas emissions down by 17 per cent from the 2005 level. The division of this overall effort between the provinces had not been negotiated. And the Canadian government announced at an international conference in Bonn, Germany, in June 2011 that it would not sign a post-Kyoto agreement. But let us take a closer look at how the post-Kyoto target of a 17 per cent reduction in emissions can be reached by 2020. An equitable (though not necessarily equal) sharing of greenhouse gas targets could reduce disparities and regional tensions. This approach, sometimes called a "European bubble," was favoured within the European Union in applying the Kyoto Protocol. Overall, the EU had to reach an 8 per cent reduction in emissions compared to 1990. But the targets were adjusted for each country to take account of its particularities. The more extreme cases were Luxembourg, down 28 per cent; Germany, down 21 per cent; Denmark, down 21 per cent; Spain, up 15 per cent; Greece, up 25 per cent; and Portugal, up 27 per cent.

Canada has not reached a consensus in this regard, with each province and the federal government choosing its own target, more or less related to the Kyoto Protocol. The main advantage in letting each province develop its own system lies in the fact that revenues from the system would remain within the province. A provincial government can use these revenues to reduce transition problems, and regional disparities are minimized. A cross-Canada system established by Ottawa could, depending on the structure adopted, result in carbon tax revenues being pocketed by the federal government (of course it could be designed so that the federal government distributes the revenues to the provinces' governments, or to their taxpayers, or otherwise within the provinces). The system's regional effect would vary according to the methods used to recycle revenues.

It should be noted that, if transfers to the provinces were in proportion to their demographic weight, as opposed to some other method, Ontario and Quebec would be favoured at the expense of Alberta and Saskatchewan. The government would thus have to balance the system by paying very close attention to regional inequalities. It would help to have an international agreement under which countries set equal and equitable requirements on their businesses and citizens.

A carbon tax, if poorly designed, risks sending a shock wave throughout the Canadian economy. When a carbon tax is implemented, great care goes into measures to ensure that companies paying the tax remain internationally competitive so as to avoid too heavy a burden. Special attention is usually paid to manufacturing and agriculture, as well as to companies with inescapably high energy needs.

To optimize a tax measure's impact, green taxes should be implemented at the right time. Between now and 2020, an entire series of green tax measures must be implemented at the right time, taking account of the supply and demand of Canadian-made green products so that the green shift by companies precedes the green shift by consumers. If green tax measures end up favouring consumption of a green product from another country because Canadian companies are not prepared for the green shift, the tax system will lead to money flowing abroad.

Canada's ecoAUTO rebate program shows the trade cost that can result from measures favouring imports. EcoAUTO was introduced in the 2007 budget speech for the period from March 20, 2007, to December 31, 2008. During this period, Ottawa encouraged Canadians to acquire 170,000 lower-pollution motor vehicles, and these came almost exclusively from Asia.

EcoAUTO was not politically necessary. What made this gaffe possible? With no experience in green shifts, governments lack a clear understanding of the optimal cycle for the implementation of green taxation. Moreover, corporate management teams and their consultants do not always grasp the ecological issues involved, and do not react quickly enough to new opportunities or to emergencies.

If Canadian companies are ready to meet the demand for green products, the government must act promptly. Undue delay may have three effects—in addition to Canada simply failing to achieve its green goals. First, taking on the mantle of social responsibility, companies would have room to make up for the government's absence and grab the green tax revenues Canadians are willing to pay. (The initiative taken by many Canadian retailers that charge extra for plastic bags to promote reusable bags is a striking example of this.) Second, measures already taken to force a green shift by businesses would be compromised. Third, the return on investments made by Canadian companies to take a green shift would be reduced.

Green taxation is both an economic and an ecological tool. Most countries that have adopted green taxation were looking initially at economic goals. Let's examine the cases of Denmark and Germany.

Denmark's Environmental Fiscal Reform, implemented during a tough economic period, was in effect a recovery plan. In 1993, the budget deficit (3.8 per cent of GDP) and the debt (80.1 per cent of GDP) were both substantial.[34] The government could no longer keep raising taxes in an effort to soak up its deficit[35] as had been done since the mid-1960s. Denmark then ranked second among OECD countries in its tax burden, with personal income tax accounting for a disproportionate share of government revenues. Its EFR was instituted with a view to cutting government spending as well as reducing personal income taxes, payroll taxes and capital taxes, in the knowledge that this would have beneficial long-term economic effects. The government also sought better control over spending by using market instruments to play part of the state role of monitoring and control.[36] Energy used for heating was highly taxed, while energy for industrial processes was taxed only lightly.[37] Tax cuts were thus offset by the increase or introduction of environmental taxes. Overall, the plan helped raise productivity by 1.5 per cent[38] and generally had a positive effect on GDP.

In Germany, the start of the EFR process coincided with a period of high unemployment following the country's reunification. It helped create jobs and increase companies' international competitiveness. In 1998, with unemployment at 12.3 per cent, compared to an average of 6.8 per cent in the other OECD countries, the decision was taken to implement an EFR aimed at increasing the use of renewable energy, spurring the development of green technologies,[39] adding jobs and thus lowering social insurance contributions. Ecological taxes apply only partially to the fishing and agricultural industries, and the manufacturing sector can get relief of up to 95 per cent. For competitive reasons, some industries benefit from favourable treatment. Without this reform, the social insurance contribution would have reached 21.2 per cent of income (instead of 19.5 per cent in 2005). From 1999 to 2005, the EFR helped create between 175,000 and 250,000 jobs and helped raise GDP by 0.1 to 0.2 per cent annually. It also had a positive effect on companies' international competitiveness by lowering the cost of energy innovations and reducing their tax burden.[40]

To get a green shift underway, action needs to be taken on several fronts at once: research and development (R&D), investment, production and consumption. The green tax bonus that I am proposing here seeks to encourage environmentally sustainable actions and attitudes in these various areas. Tax advantages related to ecological R&D need to be enhanced. Society would accept a boost of this type for organizations attempting to find solutions to environmental problems.

Current amortization rules, allowing companies to spread spending on equipment over several years, should be enhanced for the establishment of green production processes. In addition, companies should be encouraged to discard obsolete, polluting equipment through a deduction for the terminal loss of amortization on this equipment in the year they dispose of it.[41]

In environmental matters, Canada already has favourable amortization rules, including those applying to the acquisition of renewal energy production equipment.[42] In the 2009 federal budget, the government also proposed amortization rules favouring carbon capture and storage technologies. This practice is also used by other countries. For example, in the United States, the tax code allows for accelerated amortization of certain goods that help reduce air pollution.[43] Similar measures cover low-polluting vehicles in Britain and investments to fight air pollution in Finland.[44]

In addition to these measures, Canadian authorities could, at an opportune time, offer a consumption tax holiday on green products. This type of tax holiday would have little effect on the consumption habits of companies, bearing in mind the tax credits on inputs they already enjoy. However, it would give green products a competitive advantage and would maximize the return on funds invested (both public and private). It would reduce the price gap between green products and other products and would encourage the development of Canadian green products for the Canadian market. In political terms, incentives would find broader acceptance than coercive measures. Consumption tax holidays would need to be targeted carefully to avoid hurting Canadian businesses. It is important for exemptions to be brought in gradually as companies gain the ability to offer green products. Otherwise, the tax advantage would benefit foreign manufacturers.

In the last twenty years, Canada's greenhouse gas emissions have risen 25 per cent. To meet the government's announced goal of a 17 per cent reduction from 2005 levels, the shift will have to be very green—perhaps too green for voters!

Polls indicate that Canadians are asking the government to give priority to economic development, with environmental protection ranking third. In reality, no country, even among the so-called "green" countries, has agreed to treat the environment as the top priority, ahead of energy and the economy. The European Union, which sees itself as the planet's green leader, brought the post-Kyoto proposals from its member countries together in a document it called its climate and energy package. Denmark, a pioneer in imposing a carbon tax, introduced green tax reforms from 1993 to 2002, presenting environmental goals filtered through economic and financial objectives. The primary goals of Britain's green tax reform of 2001 were to secure its energy supply and maintain its companies' international competitiveness.

Fortunately, as shown by European countries as noted above, tax reforms—when carefully designed—can provide environmental, economic and financial benefits.

A REALISTIC GREEN SOLUTION

In the current Canadian context, the greenhouse gas reduction target must also satisfy economic and political requirements. Otherwise, whatever its environmental merits, any solution will remain impossible to implement. It is clear that green taxation has proven itself. But in Canada's economic, political and energy situation, instituting green taxation is only realistic if the United States makes the green shift and assumes its share of responsibility.

To pass the economic test, any reduction target must avoid negative consequences that exceed what voters are willing to pay to satisfy their ecological objectives.

To be politically feasible, a target would have to be free of any risk to the country's political stability. The problem with too ambitious a target is that it could lead to major wealth transfers from western to eastern Canada. Although Canada does not suffer from energy dependency as such, it does import the energy concerns of the United States because of its status as that country's largest and most reliable foreign supplier of oil, natural gas, electricity and uranium. In reality, the solutions chosen by Canada first require assent from the United States, because it is unlikely that the Americans would agree to any decision that puts their energy security at risk.

The most realistic solution for the moment would be to ask the United States to assume its share of responsibility for the tar sands. When he announced the 17 per cent reduction target in January 2010, then-Environment Minister Jim Prentice said that Canada was "completely aligned with the U.S. target," which also aimed at a 17 per cent cut from the 2005 level. While this announcement moderated the Canadian position, which previously had set a target of 23 per cent, two problems remain.

The 17 per cent goal is more ambitious for Canada than for the United States, because emissions in Canada have risen since 2005 while they have fallen south of the border. Since the recession led to a decline in industrial activity on the U.S. side while Canada was increasing its tar sands activity, the gap in favour of the United States may well grow wider. Between 2005 and 2008 (the latest year for which full data were available at the time of writing), Canada's emissions increased by 0.5 per cent, while the United States lowered its emissions by 2 per cent.

An equal target for both countries amounts to asking Canada to absorb the entire ecological burden of the tar sands on their own. As noted, the industry is operated primarily for Americans, who consume 80 per cent of its output, and who, moreover, are the largest foreign shareholders in the Alberta-based producers.[45]

The real (and not just nominal) gap that would exist even if both countries adopted the same 17 per cent target could cause substantial wealth transfers from north to south. This is an obvious fact, considering the mobility of capital, which would be drawn to ecologically less restrictive areas, as the United States would then be.

To remove tax inequities discriminating against Canadians,

especially those living in non-oil-producing provinces such as Ontario and Quebec, Americans would have to accept their share of responsibility for the greenhouse gas emissions caused by tar sands exploitation. Otherwise, Canada, asked unfairly to absorb the effects of American irresponsibility, would continue to take blame from the rest of the planet.

7

FIXING THE LEAKS

To put an end to the current economic crisis and to balance the books, governments will need to make major changes to our archaic tax regimes. Specifically, they are going to have to fix the tax leakage that these regimes allow. At present, trillions of dollars that should be flowing into government coffers are simply slipping away. Few would argue that government borrowing is not also a problem. Certainly debt is at the core of firmly entrenched ideologies and human behaviours in industrialized societies, and these also need to be examined.

In Canada, as in many industrialized countries, people have lived with debt financing for centuries, both personally as well as socially. At the government level, Canada has always had debt. In 1867, at the time of Confederation, Canada incurred a public debt of $76 million.[1] Starting in January 1868, the new Dominion issued $1.5 million in ten-year bonds at 6 per cent by public sale. After this initial auction, there was a second issue, and then a third and so on. Canada has borrowed almost every year, with very few exceptions; in this way, the national debt rose from $76 million to over $600 billion in less than 150 years, not counting provincial debt.

Borrowing also took place in the United States and in

almost all industrialized countries. In 1791, soon after its founding, the United States had a debt totalling $75 million. In less than 220 years, this debt increased to $15 trillion. Regardless of how sound a country's capacity to borrow is, it will not be easy to reverse centuries of public deficit financing because both citizens and their governments have become accustomed to the level of spending without taxation that debt permits.

Nevertheless, as the previous chapters in this book have shown, the current situation did not develop simply because spending is too high. Rather, it also developed because revenues are too low. Making the necessary changes to government revenues is likely to involve a long and laborious process. Some taxpayers will need to change their under-standing of taxes and specifically the definition of what a fair share of taxes involves. Changes to the basic structure of tax regimes to allow modifications that are as yet unforeseen will also be required. What may prove to be most difficult is the negotiation that will be needed to accomplish all of this within the context of global fiscal cooperation.

GLOBAL FISCAL COOPERATION

In an economy that is increasingly interconnected worldwide, fiscal policies cannot be developed in isolation. With the benefit of hindsight, we can see that it was probably a mistake to develop free trade and investment agreements without having fiscal cooperation in place. To be fully effective, any fiscal solutions to the current economic crisis will have to involve the cooperation of virtually all countries.

Countries seeking better fiscal cooperation on a global level could achieve it in several ways. One solution would be to establish a global forum that would seek comprehensive tax solutions. This would involve creating an independent body that could work either alongside existing international organizations or under the aegis of an existing organization. It would need to be separate from the OECD, which comprises only thirty-four countries, all of them industrialized. A second solution would be to create a binding global tax agreement that sets a minimum tax for signatory countries. A third solution would be to create a global economic governing body that makes binding decisions on taxation.

Countries currently engaged in working towards tax cooperation favour the second solution. As bilateral or multilateral fiscal agreements are reached, a growing number of countries are coordinating tax principles and policies. This approach allows countries to coordinate while maintaining their independence.

A new world organization that brings together all countries and is charged with the task of negotiating multilateral global tax rules will likely be needed. It should be possible to use an organization that already exists, such as the OECD, the World Bank, the IMF, the WTO or the UN. This approach would have the advantage of avoiding the costs and delays attributable to introducing a new entity. The OECD has the advantage of having played a leading role in tax cooperation for several decades, most recently with the conclusion of the multilateral convention signed November 4, 2011, in Cannes, where Secretary General Ángel Gurría said, "Today we have taken a major step towards improving tax cooperation on a global scale." On the other hand, the UN has the advantage of bringing together nearly all the world's countries.[2] In fact, the most serious discussions to date regarding the possible implementation of a global tax organization have taken place in the context of a panel of independent financial experts appointed by UN Secretary General Kofi Annan and chaired by former Mexican President Ernesto Zedillo in 2001. Alternatively, the

WTO could take the lead. In fact, it is hard to imagine how the WTO can fulfill its role of ensuring the free flow of trade and reducing nontariff barriers without having jurisdiction over tax matters.

Despite the need, global tax cooperation has many vocal critics. From governments' point of view, the reservations take two forms. First, while trade has become truly international, leading to a greater level of cross-border economic integration, the world continues to be organized politically into nation-states with sovereign governments. This leads to an inevitable degree of friction between world economic and political structures.

Second, countries are generally hesitant about the idea of tax cooperation because it is considered a threat to state sovereignty. What this argument fails to take into account is that fiscal sovereignty is already compromised because globalization forces virtually all countries to adopt competitive tax rates. In the words of Noëlle Lenoir, former French minister of European affairs and president of the Cercle des Européens, "State sovereignty is already an illusion when a company can move its tax base as it sees fit."[3]

While global tax cooperation was once viewed as a utopian concept, the economic crisis has brought it to the centre of the political debate. At the G20 summit in Cannes in November 2011, countries took an important step towards international tax cooperation by adopting a multilateral convention to fight tax evasion more effectively. The Multilateral Convention on Mutual Administrative Assistance in Tax Matters offers a wide range of tools for cross-border tax cooperation, including automatic exchange of information, multilateral simultaneous tax examinations with assistance for collecting tax debts and strong safeguards to protect the confidentiality of the information exchanged.

During the Franco-German summit in August 2011, Chancellor Angela Merkel and President Nicolas Sarkozy expressed their wish to establish a common corporate tax in Germany and France by 2013, harmonizing both the tax base and the rates. In September 2011, Belgian Finance Minister Didier Reynders suggested that the Benelux countries join the Franco-German initiative. Fiscal convergence between France and Germany poses substantial challenges, considering that Germany taxes the profits of large corporations at a rate of 15 per cent, while the rate in France is 33 per cent.

European countries have been working on the harmonization of corporate taxes for several decades. The idea was proposed in the Neumark Report in 1962 and the Van den Tempel Report in 1970. In 1992, in the Ruding Report, the European Commission proposed a minimum rate of 30 per cent, a rate far below those prevailing in the countries of the EU at the time, with the exception of Ireland and Finland. Since then, rates have fallen drastically. Between 2000 and 2011, the corporate tax rate fell from 32 per cent to 23 per cent on average among the twenty-seven EU member states.[4] In March 2011, the European Commission proposed the Directive on a Common Consolidated Corporate Tax Base, designed in particular to eliminate problems related to transfer pricing, offset cross-border losses, reduce business compliance costs and eliminate instances of double taxation. However, this initiative is not aimed at eliminating tax competition; on the contrary, the idea is to make it more transparent.

In North America, the prospect of tax harmonization seems very far down on the agenda. In fact, by lowering its corporate tax rates by half over the past decade, Canada is waging fierce competition against the United States, whose statutory corporate tax rate is 35 per cent—more than double Canada's federal rate of 15 per cent.

A GLOBAL TAX SYSTEM

To overcome the current crises, countries will need to adopt a coordinated tax plan with both long-term and short-term objectives. The long-term objective would be the establishment of a modern, fully coordinated, global tax system. Given the difficulties involved in implementing such a plan, we could not expect such a system to be in place much before 2020 at the earliest.

But the public finances of many countries around the world can no longer wait for a comprehensive, fully coordinated, global system to be phased in. They require an immediate fix. And so, the short-term objective would be the establishment of a simple, temporary tax plan to stabilize finances. This temporary tax plan would include the phased-in progression by the G20 countries (which represent approximately 85 per cent of world trade, two thirds of the world's population and more than 90 per cent of gross world product) of the following two fiscal rules:

- a minimum income tax rate of 80 per cent for the superrich, and
- a minimum income tax rate of 20 per cent for multinationals.

Let's call this the "80/20 plan."

The two hundred richest people on earth alone have the equivalent of what is available to 40 per cent of the world's population—2.46 billion people. This excessive, undertaxed and in some cases untaxed wealth creates an economic and financial imbalance. To overcome the fiscal crises we face, it is crucial that we end this unjust and inefficient distribution of global resources. Higher taxes for the wealthy could have a very significant impact in the United States and in many other countries.

A tax rate of 80 per cent for the superrich is reasonable and achievable. In fact, it is less than or comparable to what the very wealthy paid in many countries prior to the 1980s. If a minimum tax was put in place in all G20 countries, it would counter the argument that such a rule would encourage the rich to flee elsewhere.

A few superrich individuals have publicly advocated higher tax rates for the rich. According to a survey by the consulting firm Spectrem Group, 68 per cent of millionaires support raising taxes on people who earn $1 million or more in income.[5] But to date, none of them has sent a cheque, and it is unclear how much additional tax they would be willing to pay. Would the very rich be willing to pay taxes at a rate of 80 per cent? In the United States, Bill Gates said in October 2011 that he was "generally in favor of the idea that the rich should pay somewhat more"[6] than other taxpayers, and Warren Buffett explained to the *New York Times* in August 2011 that "it's time for our government to get serious about shared sacrifice."[7] But what exactly does "somewhat more" or "shared sacrifice" really mean? It is hard to know for sure.

In France, a few CEOs of leading companies—including Jean-Paul Agon of L'Oréal, Christophe de Margerie of Total and Franck Riboud of Danone—said they wanted to make an "exceptional contribution."[8] To reduce the deficit and maintain the AAA credit rating on France's debt, taxpayers whose income is between €250,000 and €500,000 a year would be subject to an extra contribution of 3 per cent, while for those who earn more than €500,000 the contribution would be 4 per cent. Some opposition parties and lobby groups see these offers as trivial ones, compared to the contribution that the superrich should be making. In Germany, the president of the Hannover soccer club, Martin Kind, and three other holders of large fortunes have declared that they are willing to pay higher taxes to reduce the debt. Another group of fifty wealthy Germans has signed a manifesto calling for the establishment of a wealth tax of 5 per cent. Meanwhile, in

Italy, a tax on the wealthiest was included in the austerity plan approved on September 14, 2011. Set at 3 per cent, it will only cover incomes above €300,000 per year.

On the campaign trail in 2008, Barack Obama and the Democrats promised not to renew the Bush administration's temporary tax reductions for the wealthiest taxpayers. They explained that these temporary reductions mainly benefit millionaires while the middle class grows poorer. The Republicans disagreed, arguing that the worst thing to do during a recession is to "raise taxes" (i.e. end the temporary reductions). In September 2011, after three years of discussions and at the risk of angering far-right Republicans, President Obama announced his firm intention not to renew the tax cuts for the rich beyond 2012. This would allow the United States to recover $800 billion over ten years.

Obama also wants to implement the "Buffett tax" and has commented that "it's math."[9] In other words, reducing the budget deficit must necessarily involve increasing taxes for the rich. A tax on millionaires will affect 450,000 U.S. taxpayers. President Obama has not indicated the specific tax rate he intends to apply or the amount he hopes to raise through this measure. According to the White House, however, it is essentially a symbolic measure with low financial impact but nevertheless necessary to ensure fairness.[10]

Yet, according to statistics compiled by the IRS for 2008, the United States could collect an additional $50 billion by taxing the 400 richest Americans (whose income totalled $91 billion) at an 80 per cent rate instead of the 21 per cent rate that actually applied.

Although this issue is virtually absent from the current policy agenda in Canada, it could become very important in the future. In 2012, Prime Minister Harper's approach relied almost exclusively on the poor and middle class to reduce the deficit. Absolutely nothing was in place to increase taxation of the superrich.

Turning from personal income tax to corporate tax, is it reasonable to enforce a minimum rate of 20 per cent for multinationals? The answer is an unqualified "yes." It is both practical and reasonable, considering that apart from tax havens and a few isolated countries—specifically, Canada, Ireland and Taiwan—the statutory tax rate applicable to corporations is universally higher than 20 per cent. In Canada, the federal statutory tax rate was lowered to 15 per cent as of January 1, 2012. Multinational corporations still pay taxes at an overall statutory rate of approximately 25 per cent, however, because they are also subject to provincial taxes. The rate has fallen to this level from 48 per cent over the past thirty years.[11] In this context, a minimum rate of 20 per cent would simply correct the system's excesses.

Finally, it is worth noting that many multinational corporations manage to reduce their tax rate to *below* 20 per cent, partly by taking advantage of tax loopholes and doing business in tax havens. Governments are seeking solutions to both these practices. The imposition of a minimum tax is a simple and readily available solution for accomplishing this goal.

The concept of a global minimum tax does not represent a threat to the public finances of countries since multinationals could not avoid being subject to that rate. Indeed, such a global minimum tax would counter multinationals' traditional claims about the need to be internationally competitive, since if a minimum rate is imposed uniformly, multinationals will be taxed at the same level.

Furthermore, the concept of international cooperation directed at establishing a minimum level of taxation is not new to countries and multinational corporations. The EU has already taken a step in this direction by requiring member countries to adopt a minimum 15 per cent rate for their value-added taxes (VAT), while applying a 5 per cent discount for some goods and services.

The vehicle for taxing multinationals at a minimum rate of 20 per cent could be a traditional income tax. Such a formula would carry a low financial risk for the multinationals since by definition they would be subject to it only if they had earned income. It would nevertheless be appropriate to consider a joint approach consisting of an income tax and a tax on financial transactions. This tax would have the advantage of being applicable without an international consensus. It would manage to tax some of the wealth otherwise sheltered in tax havens, and it would reduce the turbulence in the banking system.

Many people believe financial transactions should be taxed. A microtax on financial transactions (from 0.01 per cent to 0.1 per cent depending on the product involved) could yield at least €200 billion per year in the EU and €650 billion (about $US1 trillion) worldwide.[12]

James Tobin, a professor at Yale University in New Haven, Connecticut and 1981 Nobel laureate in economics, proposed what became known as the Tobin Tax. The idea has since been adopted by two other leading economists, 2001 Nobel laureate Joseph Stiglitz and former U.S. Treasury Secretary Lawrence Summers. The idea is to tax all foreign exchange transactions to deter speculators who convert currencies back and forth in a matter of seconds. As Tobin saw it, this would be akin to "putting a grain of sand" in these mechanisms, in the form of a very low-level tax (0.01 per cent) whose revenues would then be redistributed to the poorest countries. France, Finland, Belgium and Germany have all come out in favour of the Tobin Tax, while the United States, Canada, Switzerland, Australia, Russia and India are opposed.

A financial transaction tax is very similar to the Tobin Tax. The general idea is to introduce a tax on all transactions that present a risk to the financial system, especially speculative activities. Proposed by France and Germany, it was rejected by the G20 at its summit in Toronto in June 2010.

Shortly after this setback, France and Germany asked the European Union to revive the idea. Christine Lagarde, France's minister of economic affairs at the time and now managing director of the International Monetary Fund, said after a meeting of the twenty-seven EU finance ministers in September 2010 that a financial transaction tax "is technically feasible, practically difficult, politically desirable and financially uncertain."[13] For José Manuel Barroso, president of the European Commission, it is a question of fairness. In his speech to the European Parliament on September 28, 2011, he said that "over the last three years, member states granted aid and provided guarantees to the financial sector adding up to €4.6 trillion. It is time for the financial sector to make its contribution to society."[14]

At the G20 summit in Cannes in November 2011, the idea of a financial transaction tax earned a place on the policy agenda. Even American billionaire Bill Gates called on the G20 to consider it, although Gates acknowledged it was unlikely that member countries would agree on a worldwide financial transaction tax, explaining that "the world doesn't have one government, so you're just not going to have complete alignment on how tax structures work in all the different countries."[15]

Within the banking system, there is considerable opposition to the idea of a tax on financial transactions. Bankers argue such a tax would not stabilize markets; in reality, they fear losing their competitive edge. The United States, Canada and Britain (home to the largest European financial centre) also oppose the idea. Jean-Claude Trichet, president of the European Central Bank from 2003 to 2011, believes that such a tax would work only if it was applied globally. Yet the tax could still be applied within the euro zone, even if the commitment of all countries could not be obtained. Given the time necessary for international and multilateral negotiations, a financial transaction tax is unlikely to see the light of day before 2014.

OTHER SHORT-TERM FISCAL MEASURES

In addition to the 80/20 plan, countries should consider some other significant measures that are needed in the short term to reduce revenue leakage caused by the use of outdated tax regimes in the twenty-first century.

At the international level, proposals put forward by Canada and agreed to by other G20 countries have effectively reduced the level of protection tax evaders and avoiders enjoy in tax havens. The problem, however, is likely to remain, and it is necessary to go further. The following additional measures should be considered.

Under the current system of information exchange, countries that wish to receive information from other countries must apply by providing a taxpayer's name and address, a specified period of time and the name of the bank where the taxpayer is a customer. This information sounds as if it would be easy to get, but in reality it is very difficult for tax authorities to link taxpayers from a particular country with the names and addresses they use in tax havens. The reason is very simple: rarely would an individual who sets up a tax evasion scheme involving a tax haven do so under his or her own name. They will instead use front companies and false offices to serve as their mailbox.

To circumvent these problems, rather than relying on tax

authorities from the concerned country requesting information, as is currently the case, countries should consider the possibility of an automatic information exchange. This could be achieved in several ways. For example, the G20 countries could make sure that their financial and judicial authorities have access to files regarding all relevant establishments in tax havens, which would include information about the holdings and bank accounts of all companies.

First, taxation of multinationals can be reformed by establishing a centralized tax system or a single tax liability at the global level. This could be achieved through the kind of international tax cooperation suggested above. A centralized system of taxation for multinationals would be fairer, simpler and more efficient, and it would almost instantly eliminate unfair competition from tax havens. For political reasons, however, it would not be realistic to implement this solution in the short term, and it would not remove the problem of banking and judicial havens.

Consequently, the *reporting* or disclosure of information by country appears to be a very effective solution. It means requiring all multinationals, country by country, to report the following information: their activities in the country, the amount of their assets, the number of people they employ, ties between related persons, profits before tax and the amount of taxes paid in the country. Accounting standards constitute a powerful tool in this regard, because they make it possible to set the same rules for all international firms.

While issues relating to private charitable foundations have not really been raised in Canada, the situation is different in the United States. New York state passed a new law in August 2010 limiting tax deductions for people earning more than $10 million. It justified this new measure as follows: "The greater the tax incentives for general charitable giving, the greater the foregone revenue needed to run basic government services."[16] Overly generous tax benefits accompanying charitable donations seem to be a luxury that New Yorkers no longer wish to allow.

In his budget for fiscal year 2012, released in February 2011, President Obama proposed that taxpayers in the highest tax bracket be able to deduct charitable donations to a maximum rate of 30 per cent, down from 39.6 per cent in 2011. This is not a new idea. He had made similar proposals in 2009 and 2010. The announcement of these measures has provoked considerable controversy, and some have even accused President Obama of wanting to tax charities. Obama responded by saying he wanted to equalize things:

> Now, if it's really a charitable contribution, I'm assuming that [the tax exemption] shouldn't be the determining factor as to whether you're giving that $100 to the homeless shelter down the street. And so this provision would affect about 1 per cent of the American people. They would still get deductions. It's just that they wouldn't be able to write off 39 per cent. In that sense, what it would do is it would equalize. When I give $100, I'd get the same amount of deduction as when...a bus driver who's making $50,000 a year, or $40,000 a year, gives that same $100. Right now, he gets...to write off 28 per cent. I get to write off 39 per cent. I don't think that's fair.[17]

In his 2012 budget, President Obama also proposed a plan to simplify the way private foundations pay excise taxes on their investment income and encourage private foundations to give more. His plan would tax net investment income earned by private foundations at a flat rate of 1.35 per cent. Foundations are currently subject to a rate of 2 per cent, which in some circumstances can be reduced to 1 per cent. In June 2011, Senator Charles E. Grassley, Republican of Iowa, said that any proposed changes to the excise tax credit would require formal study and that he was not convinced that the simplification of tax rates would encourage foundations to give more.

In fact, the fundamental problem with private charitable foundations is that they are allowed to exist indefinitely. To correct this situation and to reduce the hole in public finances, an increase in the disbursement quota of 3.5 per cent in Canada (and 5 per cent in the U.S.) to 10 per cent should be considered. This would be a simple solution that would not interfere with the tax break donors receive on donations. As long as the rate of return remains below 3 per cent, a disbursement quota of 10 per cent will require the distribution of the foundation's capital over a ten- to fifteen-year period. In effect, all taxpayers finance the existence of foundations through donation tax credits. If taxpayers were assured that the contribution they make in this way would be returned to society through charitable activities within a finite period, it would make that contribution more acceptable.

As of 2012, the frozen assets held by private foundations in Canada are worth more than $20 billion. If the disbursement quota were increased from 3.5 per cent to 10 per cent, an additional $1.3 billion of these funds would be released—enough to feed most of the disadvantaged children in Canada.[18]

Even though the United States has a disbursement quota of 5 per cent, the shortfall that the system creates for the government has been acknowledged there as well, and a number of U.S. organizations have offered solutions to reduce that shortfall. For example, the National Committee for Responsive

Philanthropy, an important organization whose opinions are respected in the field, recommended in 2009 that the level of disbursement be raised from 5 to 6 per cent.[19]

With respect to electronic commerce, industrialized countries have been discussing ways of adapting tax systems to the Web since 1990, but to date none has been put in place. In the United States, for example, harmonizing tax regimes to include electronic commerce is such a politically sensitive question that a moratorium was adopted in October 1998 and then extended to 2014. On August 12, 1996, the European Commission published a report entitled *The "Bit Tax": The Case for Further Research*, which proposed taxing the transmission of information on the Web.[20] This initiative would have the advantage of minimizing the amount of useless information transmitted by the net, but the idea was rejected.

It is therefore difficult to predict what the future holds regarding taxation of electronic commerce. While waiting for a consensus on the international scale, tax authorities from individual countries must hope they will be able to manage the increasingly negative consequences arising from nontaxation of the Web.

No matter what type of tax plan is considered, it should be accompanied by environmental objectives. This is how an environmental agenda was successfully established within the tax laws in Denmark, Germany and a number of countries that are traditionally considered "green." Denmark, for example, is one of the OECD countries where green taxes are highest, standing at 4.25 per cent of GDP in 2008 compared to an OECD average of 2.18 per cent of GDP. To achieve a green shift, between 1992 and 2002 Denmark successively introduced three tax reforms that encompassed environmental goals but filtered these goals through economic and financial objectives. The Environmental Fiscal Reform of 1993, the first and most significant in terms of the changes it introduced, aimed at finding ways to lower the tax burden for Danish taxpayers who struggled with excessive tax rates and social fees on one hand and chronic deficits, high unemployment and a negative growth rate on the other. The environmental cause was sufficiently important and real in Denmark at that time to justify a new form of taxation and to allow the intro- duction of new sources of tax revenue.

However, as discussed in Chapter 6, the challenges facing a green taxation shift in Canada are substantial. When an ecological tax scheme comes up for consideration in Canada, it will be important not to underestimate those challenges.

EQUITY, EFFECTIVENESS AND SIMPLICITY

Finally, the tax system must be fair, effective and simple if it is to succeed.

Equity is the most important principle: the distribution of the tax burden must accord with each taxpayer's ability to pay. History teaches us that without equity, a taxation system is doomed to collapse sooner or later. It must be clear to citizens that they are not being asked to pay more than their fair share in taxes. The current impoverishment of the poor and middle class, widening wealth gaps and the rise of the superrich are all signs of the need to reassess the principle of equity within our tax system.

Effectiveness generally refers to the ability to optimize results or achieve high performance. In terms of fiscal policy, effectiveness is measured as the ability of a tax system to ensure revenue collection at the lowest cost and to maximize the economic benefits to the country. An effective system uses the minimum possible level of resources to operate.

Finally, *simplicity* is necessary so that citizens can under- stand their tax system and the flexibility it allows them.

This is a daunting challenge. Our current system has a fairly simple form for individuals to fill out. However, the array of deductions, credits and loopholes available to the rich and to corporations is bewildering, and provides an unfair advantage to those who can afford tax specialists to manipulate them. Beyond figures and economic theories, the current situation raises fundamental questions. The world's economy is globalized, but what about its people? Can they get together to implement genuine solutions to the current fiscal crises, and can they do it quickly enough so that the solutions will be effective? While what I've written here may seem pessimistic at times, I'm actually very optimistic about the future. Major changes will be needed to adapt our systems to the twenty-first century, and these changes will sometimes be painful. But I have confidence in human beings—in their instinct for survival and their capacity to find solutions to complex problems.

APPENDIX 1
FISCAL CRISES THROUGHOUT HISTORY

Fiscal crises are far from new. History shows that, along with religion, unfair taxes are one of the most common causes of wars, and have been the occasion for angry demonstrations and bloody revolts since ancient times. Periodically, taxpayers have felt a need to renegotiate how government spending is distributed and taxes are allocated.

In the Great Illyrian Revolt of 6 CE, people in the province of Illyria in the Balkans took up arms, refusing to pay the taxes imposed by the Roman Empire. France during the *ancien régime* also saw a succession of antitax revolts. In 1382, in the revolt known as the Harelle, the subjects of King Charles VI objected to the reinstatement of taxes on wine and salt. The king's harsh response included decapitations and an increase in taxes. The Roure revolt in 1670 saw peasants band together to attack tax agents. Intervention by King Louis XIV's army was required to put an end to the revolt. Five years later, Louis again had to send in royal troops to suppress the Stamped Paper Revolt, named after a new tax he had imposed on stamped paper.

The American and French revolutions also belong to the

great family of fiscal crises. The Boston Tea Party of 1773 marked the start of confrontations between the British government and the American colonists, leading to the American War of Independence. Upholding the principle of "no taxation without representation," the colonists wished to be represented in the Parliament at Westminster so that they could vote on issues concerning them. They were outraged by the British tax on the importation of tea into the American colonies. In protest, inhabitants of Boston disguised themselves as Natives and threw three shiploads of tea into the sea. King George III ordered the closing of Boston harbour until all the costs were reimbursed.

The French Revolution, which brought down France's absolute monarchy and resulted in significant gains for the people, was the occasion for the parliament to take control of taxes. Article 13 of the 1789 Declaration of the Rights of Man and of the Citizen stated, "A common contribution is essential for the maintenance of the public forces and for the cost of administration. This should be equitably distributed among all the citizens in proportion to their means."

Fiscal crises were less frequent in the nineteenth and twentieth centuries, as countries went into debt to forestall latent crises. But they became ubiquitous early in the twenty-first century as a number of countries faced the harsh reality of no longer being able to borrow.

Between 1999 and 2002, Argentina went through a serious economic crisis, the main causes of which were overvaluation of the peso, artificially tied to the U.S. dollar; dismantling of all customs protections and of the right to work; and a corrupt regime that benefited from privatizations and capital flight.[1] At the peak of the crisis in late 2001, a state of emergency was declared; demonstrations led to clashes with police in which several people were killed, and the public debt exceeded $140 billion (120 per cent of GDP). By 2008, the economy had recovered significantly and a new government was in place. Nevertheless, the government's fiscal choices frustrated an important category of taxpayers: farmers. To protest against higher farm taxes, they blocked roads for three weeks, hobbling the country's economy. The government did not give in to these pressures, but it did grant some benefits to small farmers.

A more violent tax revolt took place in Bolivia. In 2003, the government announced its intention to institute what became known as an *"impuestazo"*—a massive or onerous tax—of 12.5 per cent on the wages of public sector workers. This move, aimed at reducing the country's debt, was supported by the International Monetary Fund. However, taxpayers' resistance to these selective increases was underestimated. Following a popular uprising, the Bolivian government and the IMF announced that they might withdraw the *impuestazo*, but it was too late. Government repression failed to prevent conflicts between citizens and troops, which left thirteen people dead and eighty-nine injured.

APPENDIX 2

A ROUGH ESTIMATE OF THE FISCAL GAP

Canada[1]

	Amount lost (% of public revenues)
Tax havens[2] and "multi-millionaire detaxation"	3.5%–5.5%[7]
Corporate detaxation[3]	2%–3.5%
Taxation of e-commerce and private foundations[4]	0.5%–1%
TOTAL	6%–10%
Deficit – OECD countries (% of tax revenues)[5]	23% (2009)
Deficit – World (% of tax revenues)[6]	19% (2010)

APPENDIX 3

MAJOR RESTRICTIONS IMPOSED ON REGISTERED CHARITIES

To maintain their special status, registered charities must comply with laws and regulations that place significant restrictions on them.[1]

CHARITABLE PURPOSES ONLY

Registered charities cannot use their revenues to benefit their members and must devote all their resources to one of the following charitable purposes:
- the relief of poverty;
- the advancement of education;
- the advancement of religion;
- other purposes beneficial to the community in a way the courts regard as charitable.[2]

DISBURSEMENT QUOTA

The disbursement quota is the minimum amount that a registered charity must spend each year on its own charitable activities or on gifts to qualified donees. For taxation years ending after March 3, 2010, the quota is set at 3.5 per cent of the value of the charity's property that was not directly allocated to charitable activities or to administrative purposes, when the value of that property exceeds a threshold of $25,000 for a foundation or $100,000 for a charitable organization.

Qualified donees are organizations that can issue official receipts for donations.[3] They may be Canadian amateur sport associations, Canadian municipalities, the United Nations and its specialized agencies or certain foreign universities or charitable organizations.

CORPORATE CONTROL

Foundations may not acquire control of a corporation, except through a donation.[4] If they do so, they are subject to a penalty of 5 per cent (100 per cent for a repeat offence) of the amount of dividends they receive from the corporation in which they have acquired control.

COMMERCIAL ACTIVITIES

Private foundations may not engage in any business, related or otherwise.[5] Public foundations and charitable organizations may engage in business only to the extent that it is related. There are two kinds of related businesses: businesses conducted largely (more than 90 per cent) by volunteers, and related businesses that are subordinate to the purpose of the charitable organization.[6]

INVESTMENTS

Registered charities are subject to few rules regarding their investments. They must, however, operate within the disbursement quota rule, or else they risk losing their special tax status.

POLITICAL ACTIVITIES

Registered charities may engage in political activities, but these activities are very limited in type and extent.[7] There are three major restrictions:

- Activities must be entirely nonpartisan. Registered charities may not support or oppose a political party or a candidate for public office.
- Registered charities must not devote more than 10 per cent of their expenditures to political activities.
- The activities must be linked directly to the organization's charitable purposes.

BORROWING

Charitable organizations may borrow if the necessary authority is set out in their administrative regulations. Foundations may not contract debts for purposes other than current operating expenses, the purchase of investments or administrative expenses.

INTERNATIONAL ACTIVITIES

Although the law allows registered charities to conduct their own charitable activities outside Canada, this option is open only to some well-established charities that have the financial and administrative resources needed to send people abroad. A Canadian charitable organization without these resources may establish a representation agreement with an entity, usually a foreign charitable organization, which will conduct the charitable work abroad on behalf of the Canadian charity. The Income Tax Act also allows deductions and credits for donations to the United Nations or one of its specialized agencies, to prescribed foreign universities and to charitable organizations outside Canada to which the Canadian government has recently made a gift.

APPENDIX 4

MAJOR INSTRUMENTS OF GREEN TAXATION

The main instrument of green taxation consists of *ecotaxes,* or green taxes. They observe the polluter pays principle and provide for taxation of products that damage the environment. They are aimed at getting consumers to choose products that are recyclable or less polluting.

Tradable permit systems applying to carbon emissions also follow the polluter pays principle. They are a macroeconomic solution to be used concurrently with green taxes. A system of tradable permits was chosen for the purposes of the Kyoto Protocol in particular because it facilitates trading at the international level.

The tradable permit system is in harmony with the Coase theorem, which states that bargaining in the context of trade in an externality will lead to an efficient outcome, in that it enables externalities to be internalized by implementing transferable property rights regarding environmental resources. Governments create an artificial market in which economic players can exchange pollution permits. Governments must first determine the pollution tolerance threshold and distribute certificates on the basis of this threshold, either free or at auction.

Companies have an incentive to obtain rights to pollute as long as this costs less than cleanup measures. Companies that emit less pollution than the authorized quantity can sell their remaining pollution rights to other companies. Prices are then set through supply and demand. If environmental regulations become tighter, there should logically be an increase in the price of permits.[1]

Green taxes and a tradable permit system, so long as the permits are not distributed for free, produce the same result. Both create a charge for pollution. In a taxation system, government sets the price for use of a polluting substance and the market determines the quantities consumed, while in a tradable permit system the opposite applies: government sets the maximum permitted quantity for emissions, and the market sets the price.

With tradable permits, it may be hard for a polluter to determine the cost of pollution ahead of time, and this may make things tougher for management than for the taxation system. Also, environmental taxation is preferable to tradable permits when there are many widely dispersed polluters, since it applies universally, whereas emission permits would normally be limited to large entities.

However, taxpayers are more likely to accept a tradable permit system than green taxes. They feel less threatened by tradable permits and are less averse to them. One reason often invoked is that, if tradable permits are distributed for free, polluters pay only the cost of reducing emissions. With a tax on emissions, polluters must cover a cost per emission, in addition to shouldering cleanup costs. In light of all this, a system based on tradable permits is likely to become a major topic of discussion over the coming years. Barack Obama suggested implementing this type of system during the 2008 campaign and in the early part of his presidential term.

If the tradable permit system or green taxes generate substantial public revenues when implemented, this means the tax rate is not high enough. High revenues suggest that polluters prefer to pay a green tax instead of altering the way they operate. Nor is it generally advisable to apply the revenues raised through green taxes to the environment. According to the 1999 French document *Prélèvements obligatoires et environnement*,

> *Choosing a polluting activity as a base for a tax measure comes off initially as corresponding to the polluter pays principle. However, if the proceeds from a tax on a polluting substance are applied to the environment, the public resources allocated will depend on the level of pollution. Reducing activities that harm the environment will thus bring about a reduction in the resources allocated, and it can be feared that a desire to maintain the level of tax receipts could take priority over effective reduction of the pollution that is being taxed.*[2]

Unlike green taxes, other taxes are adopted to generate revenues and are normally aimed at implementing policies outside the environmental area. They assume broad tax bases and low rates of taxation. For example, certain taxes on energy and transportation do not have a primarily ecological intent, but still can have a positive impact on the environment. The revenues are generally used to repay debt, increase public investment or reduce other charges or social insurance contributions. For example, they can be used to build roads so as to reduce traffic jams.

User fees are payments for provision of a service such as electricity, water distribution, sanitation, garbage collection and disposal or industrial wastewater treatment. They are generally not included in overall government budgets because their primary aim is not to generate revenues but to cover the real cost of providing the service involved. According to a 2003 French government report,

> *In terms of taxation, a user fee may be defined as a charge involving a consideration, whereas a tax is defined as an obligatory charge without a consideration. Since pollution may be interpreted as a particular use of a natural resource (a right to pollute), a charge related to degradation of the environment may then be considered a user fee.*[3]

Tax incentives are indirect subsidies reflected in tax exemptions, refundable or nonrefundable tax credits and tax deductions. There are three arguments for why they are generally less effective than green taxes. First, they encourage the creation of new companies, which leads to a rise in pollution levels. Second, they encourage some companies to continue their activities even if they have high pollution levels that cannot be reversed. Third, they are rarely appropriate for meeting international commitments on greenhouse gas reduction since they do not guarantee any particular emission level.

Environmental Fiscal Reform (EFR) involves integrating environmental considerations, but goes beyond simply introducing green taxes. It generally includes: (1) an overhaul of existing taxes to make them more environmentally friendly; (2) elimination of environmental subsidies; (3) redistribution of revenues.

Revenue redistribution needs to be understood as a transfer of the tax burden. EFR may, in particular, reorient tax charges on employment income towards pollution or other environmentally harmful activities. EFR encourages "positive" activities and deters "negative" ones. It is a wise solution for public authorities facing a "double problem" because it provides a "double advantage." By raising taxation, EFR should help reduce environmentally harmful products and services. Also, by lightening the tax load on labour, EFR helps lower unemployment. This double advantage is indicated in the nomenclature by the term *double dividend*.

For countries dependent on energy from abroad, such as France, Germany and the United States, EFR even provides a "triple dividend." By taxing greenhouse gas-emitting products, EFR generally imposes energy discipline on citizens and helps lessen a country's energy vulnerability.

ENDNOTES

INTRODUCTION

1. "Bill Gates," *Forbes*, November 2011, retrieved from www.forbes.com/profile/bill-gates/

2. A methodology is briefly presented, but it does not include the breakdown of the calculation. See www.forbes.com/2011/03/08/world-billionaires-methodology-bylines.html

3. The 2011 financial report of Microsoft reads: "We have not provided deferred U.S. income taxes or foreign withholding taxes on temporary differences of approximately $44.8 billion resulting from earnings for certain non-U.S. subsidiaries which are permanently reinvested outside the U.S. The unrecognized deferred tax liability associated with these temporary differences is approximately $14.2 billion." Retrieved from www.microsoft.com/investor/reports/ar11/financial_review/income_taxes.html

4. Retrieved from www.nytimes.com/2011/08/16/business/buffett-calls-on-congress-to-raise-taxes-on-the-rich.html. His effective tax rates seem to be 11 per cent. See: www.forbes.com/sites/ashleaebeling/2011/11/16/tax-the-rich-state-edition/

5. The higher federal income tax rate is 35 per cent. Income tax is also charged by most U.S. states and many localities on individuals. These taxes are in addition to federal income tax and are deductible for federal tax purposes. State income tax rates vary from 1 per cent to 11 per cent of taxable income. Local governments charge income taxes generally at a lower rate (e.g. New York city charges tax at a rate that varies between 2.907 per cent to 3.648 per cent).

6. Most versions of the Facebook Statement of Rights and Responsibilities, although not the U.S. English version, note that "The website under www.facebook.com and the services on these pages are being offered to you by: Facebook Ireland Limited, Hanover Reach, 5-7 Hanover Quay, Dublin 2 Ireland'"

7. "Microsoft investit 240 millions de dollars dans Facebook, valorisé à 15 milliards," APF, 25 October 2007, retrieved from http://afp.google.com/article/ALeqM5hJTv-jgkS-HEoXuxelXJew0PHRgA

8. On November 29, 2011, *The Wall Street Journal* reported that the company is hoping that the initial public offering "IPO" would value the company at around $100 billion. Retrieved from http://online.wsj.com/article/SB100014240529702039356045770667737390883672.html

9. "In October 2006, the Bill & Melinda Gates Foundation created a two-entity structure. One entity, the Bill & Melinda Gates Foundation ('foundation'), distributes money to grantees. The other, the Bill & Melinda Gates Foundation Trust ('trust'), manages the endowment assets." (2006 annual report of the Bill & Melinda Gates Foundation, retrieved from www.gatesfoundation.org/nr/public/media/annualreports/annualreport06/AR2006Statements.html)

"The legal documents that govern the trust obligate it to fund the foundation in whatever dollar amounts are necessary to accomplish the foundation's charitable purposes. Because the foundation has the legal right to call upon the assets of the trust, the foundation's financial statements reflect an interest in the net assets of the trust in accordance with GAAP." (2010 annual report of the Bill & Melinda Gates Foundation, retrieved from www.gatesfoundation.org/annualreport/2010/Documents/2010-annual-report-ceo-letter-english.pdf)

Therefore, when analyzing if the Bill & Melinda Gates Foundation is actually spending its capital or its return on capital on charities, we also have to consider the activities in the Bill & Melinda Gates Foundation Trust ("trust"). In 2009 and 2010, the investment incomes of the trust were $4.5 and $5.8 billion respectively (2010 annual report of the Bill & Melinda Gates Foundation trust, retrieved from www.gatesfoundation.org/about/Documents/2010-trust-financial-statements.pdf). These amounts exceed the actual amounts given to charities by the Bill & Melinda Gates Foundation during these same two years; $2.47 billion in 2010 and $3.04 billion (2010 annual report of the Bill & Melinda Gates Foundation, retrieved from www.gatesfoundation.org/annualreport/2010/Documents/2010-annual-report-ceo-letter-english.pdf)

10. Valerie Strauss, "How Zuckerberg's Money is Being Spent in Newark Schools," *Washington Post*, 3 November 2011, retrieved from www.washingtonpost.com/blogs/answer-sheet/post/how-zuckerbergs-money-is-being-spent-in-newark-schools/2011/11/02/gIQADrT1gM_blog.html

11. Retrieved from http://abcnews.go.com/Technology/facebooks-zuckerberg-announces-100m-donation-schools-oprah/story?id=11718356

12. Matthew Mosk, Brian Ross and Megan Chuchmach, "Romney Parks Millions in Cayman Islands," ABC News, 18 January 2012, retrieved from abcnews.go.com/Blotter/romney-parks-millions-offshore-tax-haven/story?id=15378566

13. Vito Tanzi, "Globalization and the Work of Fiscal Termites," International Monetary Fund, *Finance & Development*, March 2001, retrieved from www.imf.org/external/pubs/ft/fandd/2001/03/tanzi.htm

14. Reuven S. Avi-Yonah, "Globalization, Tax Competition and the Fiscal Crisis of the Welfare State," working paper 113, *Harvard Law Review*, May 2000.

CHAPTER 1

1. "The Global Debt Clock," The Economist, retrieved from www.economist.com/content/global_debt_clock

2. "World," U.S. Central Intelligence Agency, *The World Factbook*, retrieved from https://www.cia.gov/library/publications/the-world-factbook/geos/xx.html

3. "The Global Debt Clock," The Economist, retrieved from www.economist.com/content/global_debt_clock

4. Systemic risk is the probability that a dysfunction will occur paralyzing the entire financial system in a large area or the whole world through interlinkages. This is a first step in process that could result in chain-reaction bankruptcies, which

would lead to a collapse of the world financial system. By contrast, nonsystemic risk describes the risks that appear when the world economy is confronted with a major external event, such as war.

5. United Nations, Department of Economic and Social Affairs, The Global Social Crisis: Report on the World Social Situation 2001 (New York: United Nations, 2011), retrieved from social.un.org/index/LinkClick.aspx?fileticket=9hX-7ka9Ad4%3d&tabid=1562

6. Ibid.

7. "Face à l'austérité, le Portugal mise sur la charité," MyEurop.info, 5 September 2011, retrieved from http://fr.myeurop.info/2011/09/05/face-a-l-austerite-le-portugal-mise-sur-la-charite-3239

8. "L'Italie adopte une taxe sur les hauts revenus," Le Monde, 12 August 2011, retrieved from www.lemonde.fr/europe/article/2011/08/12/l-italie-adopte-une-taxe-sur-les-hauts-revenus_1559172_3214.html

9. Reuters, "Crise de la dette — Italie: le Sénat approuve le plan d'austérité," Le Point.fr, 8 September 2011, retrieved from www.lepoint.fr/economie/crise-de-la-dette-italie-le-senat-approuve-le-plan-d-austerite-08-09-2011-1370962_28.php

10. David Stuckler, Sanjay Basu, Marc Suhrcke, Adam Coutts and Martin McKee, "Effects of the 2008 Recession on Health: A First Look at European Data," The Lancet, Vol. 378, Issue 9786 (9 July 2011), pp. 124–25, doi:10.1016/S0140-6736(11)61079-9

11. U.S. Government Bureau of Labor Statistics, "Employment Situation Summary," retrieved from www.bls.gov/news.release/empsit.nr0.htm

12. The principle of a debt ceiling dates back to 1917. Before that, the Treasury Department needed Congressional approval each time it wanted to sell American debt to raise funds. The establishment of a borrowing limit gave greater flexibility to the executive branch, which could now replenish the treasury without systematically going through Congress. Congress has raised the debt ceiling eight times in the last ten years.

13. For a closer look at the document, go to www.atr.org/userfiles/Congressional_pledge(1).pdf

14. Josiah Ryan, "Durbin: Constitution More Important than Grover Norquist's Taxpayer Protection Pledge," The Hill, 15 August, 2011, retrieved from thehill.com/blogs/floor-action/senate/176955-durbin-constitution-more-important-than-grover-norquists-taxpayer-protection-pledge?page=2

15. "S&P Lowers Rating of U.S. Debt to AA+," NextFinance, 7 August 2011, retrieved from www.next-finance.net/S-P-lowers-rating-of-U-S-debt-to; "Standard and Poor's dégrade la note de la dette américaine," Le Monde, 6 August 2011, retrieved from www.lemonde.fr/economie/article/2011/08/06/standard-and-poor-s-degrade-la-note-de-la-dette-americaine_1556741_3234.html

16. Jacob S. Hacker, Gregory Huber, Philipp Rehm, Mark Schelsinger and Rob Valletta, "Economic Security at Risk: Findings from the Economic Security Index," July 2010, retrieved from www.rockefellerfoundation.org/media/

download/5440db1e-a785-4248-9443-8ba5025ddc28

17. Arnaud de Borchgrave, "Debt Deal Won't Avert Credit-Rating Downgrade," Newsmax, 2 August 2011, retrieved from www.newsmax.com/deBorchgrave/Debt-credit-rating-deficit/2011/08/02/id/405824

18. "U.S. CEO Pay Jumps 11 Percent: Survey," PressTV, 9 May 2011, retrieved from www.presstv.ir/usdetail/179078.html

19. "Budget, Flaherty annonce le début d'une nouvelle ère d'austérité," Les affaires, 4 March 2010, retrieved from www.lesaffaires.com/secteurs-d-activite/gouvernement/budget--flaherty-annonce-le-debut-d-une-nouvelle-ere-d-austerite/510991

20. "World," U.S. Central Intelligence Agency, *The World Factbook.*

21. "The Global Debt Clock."

22. Raymond Bachand, Minister of Finance, Minister of Revenue and Minister Responsible for the Montreal Region, press conference, 25 October 2011.

23. *Update of Economic and Fiscal Projections*, November 8, 2001, retrieved from www.fin.gc.ca/efp-pef/2011/efp-pef-03-fra.asp#toc308266002

24. Federal taxes had decreased to 14.6 per cent of GDP from 16.2 per cent in 2005–06. The general corporate income tax rate was reduced to 15 per cent from 16.5 per cent in January 2012. This is lower than the 22 per cent rate in force in 2006 and much lower than the 35 per cent rate in the United States. The 2011 federal budget made no changes in the planned corporate income tax reductions.

25. Along the same lines, in September 2011 the OECD published a study in which it recommended that Canada eliminate some tax breaks enjoyed by businesses. It especially targeted provisions that allow companies to carry over losses incurred in one year to preceding or subsequent years. In Canada, losses eligible for carryover amounted to $210 billion in 2008, or 13.2 per cent of Canadian GDP. The OECD also pointed its finger at the complexity of carryover rules in some countries and the opportunities opened up for companies to exploit differences between the systems in different countries for purposes of "fiscal optimization." It noted the improper use of transfer pricing, transactions between entities within the same group located in different countries, complex financial instruments and even the use of accounting techniques to create "artificial" losses.

26. *Human Development Indices*, retrieved from: http://hdr.undp.org/en/media/HDI_2008_EN_Tables.pdf

27. CIA, *The World Factbook*, retrieved from: www.cia.gov/library/publications/the-world-factbook/geos/ic.html

28. Iceland's cuts involved 10 per cent of GDP over three years, while in Ireland, for example, austerity measures were aimed at bringing the deficit down from 32 per cent to 9 per cent in the course of 2011 alone.

29. "Nouveau record pour le chômage en Grande-Bretagne," Le Monde, 14 December 2011, retrieved from www.lemonde.fr/europe/article/2011/12/14/nombre-record-de-chomeurs-en-grande-bretagne_1618333_3214.html#ens_id=1569464

30. Rie Ishiguro and Kaori Kaneko, "Moody's Cuts Japan Rating, Blames Politics," Reuters, 24 August 2011, retrieved from mobile.reuters.com/article/idUSTRE77N01620110824?irpc=932

31. Yves Bourdillon, "2001–2011, la décennie BRIC," Les Échos, 1 December 2011, retrieved from www.lesechos.fr/opinions/analyses/0201770744907-2001-2011-la-decennie-bric-256646.php

32. "World," U.S. Central Intelligence Agency, The World Factbook.

33. U.S. Congressional Budget Office. The Long-Term Budget Outlook (rev. ed.), August 2010, retrieved from www.cbo.gov/ftpdocs/115xx/doc11579/06-30-LTBO.pdf

34. "Ten Trillion and Counting: Interview David Walker," Frontline, 24 March 2009, retrieved from www.pbs.org/wgbh/pages/frontline/tentrilion/interviews/walker.htm

35. Havi Echenberg, James Gauthier and André Léonard, "Some Public Policy Implications of an Aging Population," Library of Parliament, Current and Emerging Issues — 41st Parliament, retrieved from www.parl.gc.ca/Content/LOP/ResearchPublications/cei-07-e.htm

36. Ibid.

37. Ibid.

38. Committee for a Responsible Federal Budget, The Human Side of the Fiscal Crisis — Intro Keynote and Panel 1, retrieved from www.youtube.com/watch?v=WDqb09biO5o; Anne Vorce, America's Fiscal Choices at a Crossroad: The Human Side of the Fiscal Crisis, March 2011, retrieved from www.macfound.org/atf/cf/%7Bb0386ce3-8b29-4162-8098e466fb856794%7D/AMERICA%27S%20FISCAL%20CHOICES%20AT%20A%20CROSSROAD.PDF?utm_source=pubaff&utm_medium=email&utm_content=africaeducation&utm_campaign=2011-03_enews

39. Thus, the IMF blocked a loan when Ukraine decided to raise the minimum wage by 20 per cent in 2009. Similarly, in Romania, the IMF froze a €2.5 billion loan tranche scheduled for November 2009 to encourage a pay cut in the civil service, a reform of the pension system, etc.

40. Donna Smith, "Poverty Rate Hits 15-Year High," Reuters, 17 September 2010, retrieved from www.reuters.com/article/2010/09/17/us-usa-economy-poverty-idUSTRE68F4K520100917

41. "Le Canada fait piètre figure," Radio-Canada.ca, 17 September 2009, retrieved from www.radio-canada.ca/nouvelles/National/2009/09/17/002-Pauvrete-Canada-etude.shtml

42. Simon Johnson, "Fixing the Budget, and Deciding on Inequality," New York Times, 17 November 2010, retrieved from economix.blogs.nytimes.com/2010/11/17/fixing-the-budget-and-deciding-on-inequality/

43. "Washington Post-ABC News Poll," retrieved from www.washingtonpost.com/wp-srv/politics/polls/postabcpoll_060511_ATMIDNIGHT.html

44. OECD Tax Statistics, 2010 (Paris: OECD); OECD National Accounts

Statistics, 2010 (Paris: OECD). Retrieved from http://stats.oecd.org/Index. aspx?DataSetCode=NAAG_2010

45. OECD Tax Statistics, 2010.

46. Reuven S. Avi-Yonah, "Globalization, Tax Competition and the Fiscal Crisis of the Welfare State," working paper 113, *Harvard Law Review*, May 2000.

47. Vito Tanzi, « Globalization and the Work of Fiscal Termites, » International Monetary Fund, *Finance & Development*, March 2001, retrieved from www.imf. org/external/pubs/ft/fandd/2001/03/tanzi.htm

48. Michael J. Graetz, "Taxing International Income — Inadequate Principles, Outdated Concepts, and Unsatisfactory Policy," Yale Law School, Faculty Scholarship Series, Paper 1618 (2001), retrieved from digitalcommons.law.yale.edu/ fss_papers/1618

49. See Appendix 2.

50. In a progressive tax system, as income rises, so does the proportion of income paid in taxes. This is clearly the fairest way of proceeding: the lower the income, the greater the risk that a tax levy, even a minimal one, will interfere with the satisfaction of basic needs. Nevertheless, progressive taxation is a recent innovation, and hasn't really been in place since after the Second World War. In France, it is implemented through the income tax, the solidarity tax on wealth (ISF) and the succession tax.

51. Guillaume Duval, "Un système fiscal de plus en plus injuste," Alternatives Économiques, 8 July 2010, retrieved from www.alternatives-economiques.fr/ un-systeme-fiscal-de-plus-en-plus-injuste_fr_art__48832.html

52. Ibid.

53. Armine Yalnizyan, *The Rise of Canada's Richest 1%* (Ottawa: Canadian Centre for Policy Alternatives, 2010), retrieved from www.policyalternatives.ca/sites/ default/files/uploads/publications/National%20Office/2010/12/Richest%201%20 Percent.pdf

54. Ibid.

55. The Economic Policy Institute is a nonprofit organization that promotes the economic and political interests of low- and middle-income workers (www.epi.org).

56. Bain & Company, "Number of Chinese High Net Worth Individuals Nearly Doubles Since Onset of Global Recession, According to Far-Reaching '2011 China Private Wealth Study,'" 19 April 2011, retrieved from www.bain.com/about/press/ press-releases/number-of-chinese-high-net-worth-individuals.aspx

57. France, Institut National de la Statistique et des Études Économiques, Les revenus et le patrimoine des ménages — Insee Références — Édition 2010 (Paris, 2010), summary retrieved from www.insee.fr/fr/themes/document.asp?reg_ id=0&ref_id=REVPMEN10a

58. Steven Thomma, "Poll: Best Way to Fight Deficits: Raise Taxes on the Rich," McClatchy Newspapers, 18 April 2011, retrieved from www.mcclatchydc. com/2011/04/18/112386/poll-best-way-to-fight-deficits.html

59. Bruce Bartlett, "Tax the Rich: The Battle Cry Paul Ryan Rejects," Fiscal Times, 22 April 2011, retrieved from www.thefiscaltimes.com/Columns/2011/04/22/Tax-the-Rich-The-Battle-Cry-Paul-Ryan-Rejects.aspx?p=1

60. Warren E. Buffett, "Stop Coddling the Super-Rich," 14 August 2011, Retrieved from www.nytimes.com/2011/08/15/opinion/stop-coddling-the-super-rich.html

61. His effective tax rates seem to be 11 per cent. See: www.forbes.com/sites/ashleaebeling/2011/11/16/tax-the-rich-state-edition/

62. OECD, Tax Reform Trends in OECD Countries, Paris, 30 June 2011, retrieved from www.oecd.org/dataoecd/9/23/48193734.pdf

63. OECD, Revenue Statistics, 2010.

64. Most versions of the Facebook Statement of Rights and Responsibilities, although not the U.S. English version, note that "The website under www.facebook.com and the services on these pages are being offered to you by: Facebook Ireland Limited, Hanover Reach, 5-7 Hanover Quay, Dublin 2 Ireland"

65. "Microsoft investit 240 millions de dollars dans Facebook, valorisé à 15 milliards," AFP, 25 October 2007, retrieved from afp.google.com/article/ALeqM5hJTv-jgkS-HEoXuxelXJew0PHRg

66. On November 29, 2011, the Wall Street Journal reported that the company is hoping that the initial public offering "IPO" would value the company at around $100 billion. Retrieved from http://online.wsj.com/article/SB10001424052970203935604577066773790883672.html

67. Compared to a fortune estimated to be $17.5 billion.

68. Bianca Bosker, "Mark Zuckerberg Opens up on Oprah (VIDEO): His Home, Relationship, and Major Donation," Huffington Post, 24 September 2010, retrieved from www.huffingtonpost.com/2010/09/24/mark-zuckerberg-oprah-vid_n_738468.html

69. Valerie Strauss, "How Zuckerberg's Money is Being Spent in Newark Schools," Washington Post, 3 November 2011, retrieved from www.washingtonpost.com/blogs/answer-sheet/post/how-zuckerbergs-money-is-being-spent-in-newark-schools/2011/11/02/gIQADrT1gM_blog.html

70. Forbes, March 2011.

71. Retrieved from: www.bloomberg.com/apps/news?pid=newsarchive&sid=aAKluP7yIwJY

72. "Irlande: HP, Google et Microsoft s'opposent à une hausse d'impôt," Yahoo France Actualités, 23 November 2010, retrieved from fr.news.yahoo.com/irlande-hp-google-microsoft-sopposent-%C3%A0-hausse-dimp%C3%B4t.html

73. Jesse Drucker, "Google 2.4 Rate Shows how 60 Billion Lost," 21 October 2010, retrieved from www.bloomberg.com/news/2010-10-21/google-2-4-rate-shows-how-60-billion-u-s-revenue-lost-to-tax-loopholes.html

74. Microsoft corporation, 2011 annual report, retrieved from www.microsoft.com/investor/reports/ar11/financial_review/income_taxes.html

75. Ibid.

76. "Bill Gates: 'I'm Generally in Favor of the Rich Paying More in Taxes,'" ThinkProgress, 30 October 2011, retrieved from thinkprogress.org/economy/2011/10/30/356718/bill-gates-im-generally-in-favor-of-the-rich-paying-more-in-taxes/; "Bill Gates: I Support Taxing the Rich More than the Poor," *Huffington Post*, 31 October 2011, retrieved from www.huffingtonpost.com/2011/10/31/bill-gates-says-he-supports-taxing-the-rich_n_1067079.html

77. Based on an article published by Bloomberg on September 2011, Microsoft has retained Timothy E. Punke to lobby the repatriation tax holiday. Retrieved from www.bloomberg.com/news/2011-09-29/google-joins-apple-mobilizing-lobbyists-to-push-for-tax-holiday-on-profits.html

78. Or to the Bill & Melinda Gates Foundation Trust.

79. The foundation's website (www.gatesfoundation.org) notes, "Based in Seattle, Washington, the foundation is led by CEO Jeff Raikes and Co-chair William H. Gates Sr., under the direction of Bill and Melinda Gates and Warren Buffett."

80. And the Bill & Melinda Gates Foundation Trust.

81. "Bill Gates invite le G20 à augmenter l'aide aux pays pauvres," RIA Novosti, 3 November 2011, retrieved from fr.rian.ru/business/20111103/191812747.html

CHAPTER 2

1. This chapter is based in part on a study that I carried out in 2006 at Harvard's Kennedy School of Government.

2. The Economic Policy Institute is a nonprofit organization that promotes the economic and political interests of low- and middle-income workers (www.epi.org).

3. "Clinton, Chine et ZIRP: les germes de la crise," 3 February 2009, retrieved from www.dailybourse.fr/analyse-Clinton-Chine-et-ZIRP-les-germes-de-la-crise-vtptc-7290.php

4. OECD, *Tax Reform Trends in OECD Countries*, retrieved from www.oecd.org/dataoecd/9/23/48193734.pdf

5. Kristian Wiese, "Corporate Tax Warning," *OECD Observer*, May 2007, retrieved from www.oecdobserver.org/news/fullstory.php/aid/2229/Corporate_tax_warning.html

6. Kevin A. Hassett and Eric M. Engen, "Does the U.S. Corporate Tax Have a Future ?", 8 November 2002, retrieved from www.aei.org/files/2002/11/08/Does%20the%20US%20Corporate%20Tax%20Have%20a%20Future.pdf

7. Thomas Piketty, "Le désastre irlandais," Libération, 14 April 2009, retrieved from piketty.pse.ens.fr/fichiers/presse/LIBERATION2_090414.html

8. Ulrika Lomas, "Greece brings forward corporate tax cuts," Tax-News.com, 16 September 2010, retrieved from www.tax-news.com/news/Greece_Brings_Forward_Corporate_Tax_Cuts_45339.html

9. Harry Papachristou, "Greek PM Offers Some Tax Relief," 11 September 2011, retrieved from http://ca.reuters.com/article/idCATRE6895L920100911

10. Retrieved from http://www.rtbf.be/info/monde/detail_a-limerick-les-sinistres-de-dell-essaient-toujours-de-s-en-sortir?id=6022113

11. "The European Globalisation Adjustment Fund (EGF) aims to support redundant workers, mainly in regions and sectors which have been disadvantaged by exposure to the globalised economy. It has a potential annual budget of EUR 500 million to facilitate the reintegration into employment of workers." Retrieved from http://europa.eu/legislation_summaries/employment_and_social_policy/social_agenda/c10155_en.htm

12. Retrieved from http://europa.eu/rapid/pressReleasesAction.do?reference=IP/09/1348&format=HTML&aged=1&language=EN&guiLanguage=fr

13. Tiebout, C. A Pure Theory of Local Expenditures // *The Journal of Political Economy.*—1956.—Vol.64.—#5.—P. 416—424.

14. Additional criteria such as banking secrecy, limited shareholder liability and legislative arrangements can also sometimes carry significant weight, and some specialists suggest that it should be possible to turn these factors to direct financial advantage.

15. Kristian Wiese, "Corporate Tax Warning," *OECD Observer*, May 2007, retrieved from www.oecdobserver.org/news/fullstory.php/aid/2229/ Corporate_tax_warning.html

16. Foreign direct investment is defined as the "functional classification in the financial account of the balance of payments and in the international investment position which refers to an investment of a resident entity in one country obtaining a lasting interest in an enterprise resident in another country. The lasting interest implies the existence of a long-term relationship between the direct investor and the enterprise and a significant degree of influence by the investor on the management of the enterprise" (www.statcan.gc.ca/nea-cen/gloss/bp-eng.htm).

17. Department of Finance, *Tax Expenditures and Evaluations* 2008: 4, "Part 2: Research Report: Considerations in Setting Canada's Corporate Income Tax Rate," retrieved from www.fin.gc.ca/taxexp-depfisc/2008/taxexp08_4-eng.asp

18. OECD, *Revenue Statistics*, 1965–2008 (OECD, 2009).

19. Ibid.

20. Kristian Wiese, "Corporate Tax Warning," *OECD Observer*, May 2007, retrieved from www.oecdobserver.org/news/fullstory.php/aid/2229/ Corporate_tax_warning.html

21. Reuven S. Avi-Yonah, "Globalization, Tax Competition, and the Fiscal Crisis of the Welfare State," *Harvard Law Review*, Vol. 113, No. 7 (May 2000), pp. 1573–1676.

22. OECD, *Revenue Statistics*, 1965–2009.

23. OECD, *Revenue Statistics*, 1965–2009.

24. Retrieved from www.imf.org/external/pubs/ft/fm/2011/02/pdf/fm1102.pdf

25. Retrieved from www.imf.org/external/pubs/ft/scr/2011/cr11351.pdf

26. Leon Bettendorf, Joeri Gorter and Albert van der Horst, "Who Benefits from

Tax Competition in the European Union?", CPB Netherlands Bureau for Economic Policy Analysis, document 125, August 2006.

27. The share of corporate taxes in Greece's public finances fell from 12 per cent in 2000 to 8 per cent in 2007, according to the *Revenue Statistics, 1965–2007*, compiled by the OECD (2008).

28. "Hot Money," *Business Week*, 20 March 1995.

29. Retrieved from www.working-minds.com/TJquotes.htm

30. Trilateralism: the Trilateral Commission and elite planning for world management, Holly Sklar, South End Press (1 July 1999).

31. OECD, *Revenue Statistics, 1965–2009*.

CHAPTER 3

1. James Doran, "Madoff Probe Focuses on Tax Havens," 28 December 2008, retrieved from www.guardian.co.uk/business/2008/dec/28/bernard-madoff-fraud-investigation-offshore

2. Group of Twenty, Declaration on Strengthening the Financial System, *London*, 2 April 2009, retrieved from www.g20.org/Documents/Fin_Deps_Fin_Reg_Annex_020409_-_1615_final.pdf

3. Retrieved from http://ccfd-terresolidaire.org/e_upload/pdf/BilanpolitiqueparadisfiscauxG20ver_comp.pdf?PHPSESSID=6a02a76231e63b3c8bf20fa109d4dfe5

4. The most important economic research organization in the United States, including 16 Nobel laureates in economics among its associates.

5. Dhammika Dharmapala and James R. Hines Jr., "Which Countries Become Tax Havens?", U.S. National Bureau of Economic Research, Working Paper no 12802, December 2006, retrieved from www.nber.org/papers/w12802

6. Ronen Palan, Global Political Economy: Contemporary Theories (London and New York: Routledge, 2000).

7. Nellie Cardinale, *Chile: Education and Neoliberal Economic Policies*, retrieved from www.oecd.org/document/1/0,3746 ,fr_21571361_43854757_45626113_1_1_1_1,00.html

8. "La liste des paradis fiscaux," 21 February 2012, retrieved from www.fb-bourse.com/liste-ocde-paradis-fiscaux-2009/

9. Retrieved from www.oecd.org/document/57/0,374 ,en_2649_33745_30578809_1_1_1_1,00.html

10. Retrieved from www.oecd.org/document/36/0,3746 ,fr_21571361_43854757_45623012_1_1_1_1,00.html

11. Reuters, "REFILE-Canadian Probe into Tax Cheats Hits Snag at UBS," 5 January 2010, retrieved from www.reuters.com/article/idUSN054563520100105

12. CIA, *The World Factbook*, retrieved from https://www.cia.gov/library/publications/the-world-factbook/geos/xx.html

13. Ann Hollingshead, *Privately Held, Non-Resident Deposits in Secrecy Jurisdictions*, Global Financial Integrity, March 2010, retrieved from www. gfintegrity.org/storage/gfip/documents/reports/gfi_privatelyheld_web.pdf

14. Martin A. Sullivan, *Offshore Explorations: Jersey*, Tax Analysts, 23 October 2007, retrieved from www.taxanalysts.com/www/features.nsf/Articles/3ACC6C4D1 B6B00218525738A006716E4?OpenDocument

15. Hedge Fund Research Inc., "HFR Industry Report—Year End 2006," retrieved from www.hedgefundresearch.com

16. Tax Justice Network, "The Price of Offshore," March 2005, retrieved from www.taxjustice.net/cms/upload/pdf/Price_of_Offshore.pdf

17. United States Senate Permanent Subcommittee on Investigations, *Tax Haven Banks and U.S. Tax Compliance*, report, 17 July 2008, retrieved from hsgac.senate. gov/public/_files/071708PSIReport.pdf

18. Oxfam International, "Tax Haven Crackdown Could Deliver $120bn a Year to Fight Poverty," 13 March 2009, retrieved from www.oxfam.org/en/pressroom/ pressrelease/2009-03-13/tax-haven-could-deliver-120bn-year-fight-poverty

19. BBC News, "Q&A: Northern Rock and Granite," 21 February 2008, retrieved from news.bbc.co.uk/2/hi/business/7256431.stm

20. Greg Gordon, "How Goldman Secretly Bet on the U.S. Housing Crash," McClatchy Newspapers, 1 November 2009, retrieved from www.mcclatchydc. com/2009/11/01/77791/how-goldman-secretly-bet-on-the.html

21. Scott Klinger, Chuck Collins and Holly Sklar, *Unfair Advantage: The Business Case Against Overseas Tax Havens, Business and Investors Against Tax Haven Abuse*, 20 July 2010, retrieved from businessagainsttaxhavens.org/wp-content/ uploads/2010/07/TaxHaven.pdf

22. Angel Gurría, "The Global Dodgers," *The Guardian*, 27 November 2008, retrieved from www.guardian.co.uk/commentisfree/2008/nov/27/comment-aid-development-tax-havens

23. Valérie de Senneville, "Liste HSBC: l'informateur du fisc français sort du silence," *Les Échos*, 18 February 2009, retrieved from www.lesechos.fr/patrimoine/ banque/300398613.htm

24. Élisabeth Eckert and Pierre-Yves Frei, "L'affaire du vol chez HSBC se corse," *24 heures*, 14 December 2009, retrieved from www.24heures.ch/actu/economie/affaire-vol-hsbccorse-2009-12-14

25. Jean-Noël Cuénod, "Sarkozy cautionne l'utilisation des documents volés à HSBC," *24 heures*, 14 December 2009, retrieved from www.24heures.ch/ node/133093

26. Robert Watts, Matthew Campbell and Nicola Smith, "Revenue Men Prise Open Princely Tax Haven, Liechtenstein," London *Sunday Times*, 24 February 2008, retrieved from www.timesonline.co.uk/tol/money/tax/article3423428.ece

27. Mike Esterl, Glenn R. Simpson and David Crawford, "Stolen Data Spur Tax Probes Ex-Staffer of Bank in Liechtenstein Offered Information," *Wall Street Journal*, 19 February 2008, p. A4; Eric Pfanner and Mark Landler, "Liechtenstein

Defends Its Banks in German Tax-Evasion Inquiry," *New York Times*, 19 February 2008, retrieved from www.nytimes.com/2008/02/19/business/worldbusiness/19iht tax.4.10198813.html?_r=1

28. Retrieved from www.parl.gc.ca/HousePublications/Publication.aspx?DocId=48 84671&Mode=1&Parl=40&Ses=3&Language=E

29. Robert E. Lipsey, "Measuring the Location of Production," Working paper 14121, 21 February 2012, retrieved from www.nber.org/papers/w14121.pdf

30. Pascal Canfin, "Panorama des paradis fiscaux," *Alternatives économiques*, No. 290 (April 2010), retrieved from www.alternatives-economiques.fr/panorama-des-paradisfiscaux_fr_art_916_48748.html

31. "Senator Probes Deepwater Horizon Owner's Taxes" CBS News, 30 June 2010, retrieved from www.cbsnews.com/stories/2010/06/30/business/main6634939.shtml

32. Christian Chavagneux, "Mondialisation: les multinationales adorent les paradis fiscaux," *Alternatives économiques*, No. 272 (September 2008), retrieved from www. alternatives-economiques.fr/index.php?ogn=MODNL_80&prov=&cat=&lg=fr &id_article=38286.html

33. Le MagIT, "Bloomberg démonte les mécanismes d'optimisation fiscale de Google," Channelnews.fr, 25 October 2010, retrieved from www.channelnews.fr/ expertises/28/7987-bloomberg-demonte-les-mecanismes-doptimisation-fiscale-degoogle-.html

34. "Pionniers contre la fraude fiscale," *Observateur OCDE*, retrieved from www. observateurocde.org/m/fullstory.php/aid/2848/Pionniers_contre_la_fraude_fiscale. html

35. Fiscal transparency was a key topic of discussion at the G20 summits in Washington (November 2008), London (April 2009) and Pittsburgh (September 2009).

36. OECD, "Spain 2011: DAC Peer Review, Main Findings and Recommendations," retrieved from www.oecd.org/document/57/0,3746 ,en_2649_33745_30578809_1_1_1_1,00.html

37. OECD, "Business Innovation Policies: Selected Country Comparisons," retrieved from www.oecd.org/document/51/0,3746 ,en_21571361_43854757_47572915_1:_1_1_1,00.html

38. OECD, "The Multilateral Convention on Mutual Administrative Assistance in Tax Matters," retrieved from www.oecd.org/dataoecd/63/62/48978955.pdf

39. Retrieved from http://eur-lex.europa.eu/LexUriServ/LexUriServ.do?uri=OJ:L:2 003:157:0038:0048:fr:PDF

40. There have been transitional rules applying to Belgium, Luxembourg and Austria, although the directive does give them the right to receive information from other governments. The directive, based on the system of withholding funds at source, requires that when the effective beneficiary lives in a different country from the agent paying the interest, Belgium, Luxembourg and Austria withhold at source 15 per cent during the first three years of the transition period, 20 per cent during the next three years and 35 per cent thereafter. It should be noted that since January 2010 Belgium has opted to introduce automatic information exchange.

41. The Commission drafts bills for the European Parliament, implements EU policies and manages the European budget. It also monitors compliance with EU treaties and legislation.

42. European Commission, Taxation and Customs Union, "Common Tax Base," retrieved from ec.europa.eu/taxation_customs/taxation/company_tax/common_tax_base/index_en.htm

43. Christian Chavagneux, Richard Murphy and Ronen Palan, "Les paradis fiscaux: entre évasion fiscale, contournement des règles et inégalités mondiales," *L'Économie politique* no. 042 (April 2009), retrieved from www.alternatives-economiques.fr/les-paradis-fiscaux--entre-evasion-fiscale--contournement-des-regles-et-inegalites-mondiales_fr_art_836_42965.html

44. European Commission, Taxation and Customs Union, "Common Tax Base."

45. IRS, "Qualified Intermediaries," retrieved from www.irs.gov/businesses/corporations/article/0,,id=150934,00.html

46. IRS, "Summary of Key FATCA Provisions," retrieved from www.irs.gov/businesses/corporations/article/0,,id=236664,00.html

47. IRS, "Treasury and IRS Issue Guidance Outlining Phased Implementation of FATCA," retrieved from www.irs.gov/newsroom/article/0,,id=242164,00.html

48. Canada Revenue Agency, "Utiliser des paradis fiscaux pour ne pas payer d'impot," retrieved from www.cra-arc.gc.ca/F/pub/tg/rc4507/rc4507-09f.pdf

49. Canada Revenue Agency, *Using Tax Havens to Avoid Paying Taxes: Worth the Risk?*, retrieved from www.cra-arc.gc.ca/E/pub/tg/rc4507/rc4507-09e.pdf

50. Subject to provisions in applicable tax conventions, when a nonresident sells shares in Canadian companies, section 116 of the Income Tax Act called for a Canadian buyer temporarily to withhold between 10 per cent and 25 per cent of the price paid to the nonresident. The 2010–11 federal budget eliminates this obligation. The government abolished this obligation for the sale of Canadian shares by nonresidents in most industrial sectors (apart from real estate, mining and forestry).

51. Alain Deneault and Claude Vaillancourt, "Accord de libre-échange entre le Canada et le Panama," Mondialisation.ca, 29 December 2010, retrieved from mondialisation.ca/index.php?context=va&aid=22554

CHAPTER 4

1. Thank you to Sylvie Therrien, a specialist in sales taxes at the firm Amyot Gélinas. Mme Therrien verified some of the technical aspects of this chapter in relation to the application of sales taxes in Quebec and Canada.

2. "L'impact du développement d'Internet sur les finances de l'État," a report commissioned by the French Senate and made public in 2009.

3. Hugo Fontaine, "Le fisc 's'en vient' sur eBay," *La Presse Affaires*, 31 July 2009, retrieved from lapresseaffaires.cyberpresse.ca/economie/technologie/200907/31/01-888683-le-fisc-sen-vient-sur-ebay.php

4. European Commission, *A Digital Agenda for Europe*, 19 May 2010, retrieved from http://ec.europa.eu/information_society/digital-agenda/documents/digital-agenda-communication-en.pdf

5. Statistics Canada, "Canadian Internet Use Survey," *The Daily*, 10 May 2010, retrieved from www.statcan.gc.ca/daily-quotidien/100510/dq100510a-eng.htm

6. Ecommerce-land, "History of Ecommerce," retrieved from www.ecommerce-land.com/history_ecommerce.html›

7. Walter Hellerstein, *Electronic Commerce and the Challenge for Tax Administration*, 2 May 2001, retrieved from unpan1.un.org/intradoc/groups/public/documents/un/unpan001065.pdf

8. See OECD, "Internet Economy" (www.oecd.org/about/0,3347 ,en_2649_37441_1_1_1_1_37441,00.html). At the Ottawa meeting, the OECD established principles that should guide taxation of electronic commerce: neutrality (taxation should be neutral across different forms of electronic commerce and traditional commerce, and especially avoid double taxation); efficiency (costs should be minimized for companies and tax authorities); clarity and simplicity (tax rules should be clear and easy to understand); reliability and fairness (it should be possible to collect the right amount of tax at the right time, and opportunities for tax evasion should be minimized); and flexibility (the tax system should be flexible and dynamic so that technological and commercial developments can be taken into account).

9. In April 1998, the Minister's Advisory Committee on Electronic Commerce published a report in which it made general recommendations regarding the way in which the Department of National Revenue should establish tax rules for electronic commerce. In May 1999, the department established four Technical Advisory Groups (TAGs) to provide expert advice regarding electronic commerce. The TAGs cover the following areas: taxpayer services, consumption taxes, interpretation and international cooperation, and administration and compliance with the law. Each TAG works on developing practical recommendations for applying tax rules to electronic commerce.

10. Marie-Catherine Beuth, "Taxe Google: Le CNN soumet ses propositions à Bercy," *Le Figaro*, 15 June 2011, retrieved from www.lefigaro.fr/medias/2011/06/15/04002-20110615ARTFIG00564-taxe-google-le-cnn-soumet-ses-propositions-a-bercy.php

11. Stéphane Hayeur, "La notion d'établissement stable et le commerce électronique," *Revue* de l'Association de Planification Fiscale et Financière, 2nd quarter 2003.

12. In 2001, members of the OECD Committee on Fiscal Affairs arrived at a consensus regarding interpretation of the concept of permanent establishment for the purposes of electronic commerce. The four main elements of the consensus are: (1) A website cannot in itself constitute a permanent establishment; (2) in general, an agreement providing for hosting a website does not lead to the existence of a permanent establishment for the company that carries on commercial activities through this site; (3) an Internet service provider does not, other than under very exceptional circumstances, constitute a dependent agent of another company

so as to constitute a permanent establishment of that company; and (4) while a place where computer equipment, such as a server, can in some circumstances constitute a permanent establishment, that is true only if the operations carried out in that place are significant and constitute an essential element of the company's commercial activity.

13. Mario Charrette, "Commerce électronique: des milliers d'emplois en perspective," *Métro*, 1 April 2009, retrieved from www.journalmetro.com/Carrieres/article/205823

14. Retrieved from www.lesaffaires.com/archives/les-affaires/le-quebec-en-voie-de-perdre-la-bataille-du-commerce-electronique/510682

15. Quebec Law Network, "Le commerce électronique, les taxes et l'impôt, une zone grise?", 16 March 2000, retrieved from www.avocat.qc.ca/affai res/iiecommerce-sbdt.htm

16. Mukesh Arya, "Auditing E-Taxation," retrieved from www.intosaiitaudit. org/intoit_articles/18p36top41.pdf

17. *eBay Canada Ltd.* v. *Minister of National Revenue* (2008 FCA 141).

18. Alexandra Brown and Pooja Samtani, "Requirement to Disclose Third-Party Information: eBay Canada Ruling Raises the Stakes," Canadian Bar Association, *National* Magazine's *Addendum*—Business and Corporate Edition, February 2009, retrieved from www.cba.org/CBA/newsletters-addendum/2009/2009-02_bc.aspx

19. From a legal point of view, it was not logical to consider that the information was located outside Canada for the purposes of section 231.6 of the Income Tax Act.

20. The CRA could require that the information be provided under section 231.2 of the act rather than under section 231.6.

21. "Le PDG de Google prédit la fin de l'anonymat sur Internet," *Le Monde*, 5 August 2010, retrieved from www.lemonde.fr/technologies/article/2010/08/05/le-pdg-de-google-predit-la-fin-de-l-anonymat-sur-internet_1396083_651865.html

22. Brown and Samtani, "Requirement to Disclose Third-Party Information."

CHAPTER 5

1. The Rockefeller Foundation was established in 1913 by John D. Rockefeller, Sr., with about $100 million from the family fortune. Currently headed by Judith Rodin, the Rockefeller Foundation has assets of approximately $3 billion, and it injects more than $100 million annually into a number of sectors. The foundation has provided substantial assistance in the health field, contributed to preserving documentation through the creation of the Rockefeller Archive Center, and participated in the development of schools for African Americans at a time when such schools were practically nonexistent.

2. National Center for Charitable Statistics (NCCS), "Number of Private Foundations in the United States, 2010" (nccsdataweb.urban.org/PubApps/profileDrillDown. php?state=US&rpt=PF). See also nccs.urban.org/index.cfm

3. Canada Revenue Agency, Charities Directorate.

4. MasterCard Foundation, "FAQs," retrieved from www.mastercardfdn.org/pdfs/Fact%20Sheet%20-%20FAQs.pdf

5. Tonda MacCharles, "G8 Commitment to Poor Mothers and Children Not Nearly Enough, Critics Say," Toronto *Star*, 26 June 2010, retrieved from www.thestar.com/news/canada/article/828582--canada-to-pledge-1b-in-new-cash-for-maternal-health

6. The Bill & Melinda Gates Foundation merged with the William Henry Gates II Foundation, then headed by Bill Gates's father, in 2000.

7. Bill & Melinda Gates Foundation, "Foundation Fact Sheet," retrieved from www.gatesfoundation.org/about/Pages/foundation-fact-sheet.aspx

8. Andre Tartar, "IKEA Foundation is World's Richest 'Charity,'" *Suite 101*, November 29, 2009, retrieved from www.suite101.com/content/ikea-foundation-is-worlds-richest-charity-a174998; "IKEA Shelters its Enormous Profits from Tax via World's Biggest 'Charity,'" *Tax Prof Blog*, retrieved from taxprof.typepad.com/taxprof_blog/2010/01/how-ikea-shelters.html; "IKEA: Flat-Pack Accounting: Forget About the Gates Foundation; The World's Biggest Charity Owns IKEA — and is Devoted to Interior Design," *The Economist*, 11 May 2006, retrieved from www.economist.com/node/6919139?story_id=6919139

9. The J. W. McConnell Foundation is a private family foundation that funds programs aimed at encouraging a more innovative, inclusive, sustainable and resilient society. The foundation has undertaken or launched initiatives in education, the arts, community development, sustainability and health. Registered as a charitable organization since 1967, it currently has assets of $485,221,582, with an operating budget of $19,121,653. It disbursed $14,644,182 in 2010, and has thirteen full-time and three part-time employees.

In 2006, the celebrated billionaire Warren Buffett, who made his fortune in finance, pledged shares worth approximately $31 billion to the Gates Foundation. Buffett's donation makes it possible for the foundation to spend some $3 billion annually to accomplish its mission.

The Ford Foundation was established in 1936 in Detroit by Edsel Ford, Henry Ford's son. The foundation's current president is Luis Ubiñas and its head office is in New York. It has assets of about US$10 billion, issues grants of almost half a billion dollars annually and supports a number of cultural sectors including visual arts, theatre and music. In 2009 the Ford Foundation donated $300,000 to the Wikimedia Foundation, which provides financial aid to organizations using the MediaWiki free open source wiki software package.

In England, the Wellcome Trust, with assets of £14 billion (more than US$20 billion), supports "the brightest minds in biomedical research and the medical humanities" with a view towards achieving "extraordinary improvements in human and animal health." Established in 1936 through a provision in the will of Henry Wellcome, founder of a major pharmaceutical multinational, it is one of the largest charitable organizations in Britain, with annual expenditures of more than £720 million.

With a fortune valued at $13.3 billion, Azim Premji is nicknamed the "Indian Bill Gates." His powerful foundation has operated since 2001 and focuses primarily on education in India. The Azim Premji Foundation supports 2.5 million children in at least 13,000 schools.

In Hong Kong, the Li Ka Shing Foundation (LKSF) bears the name of its founder, a leading businessman who chairs Cheung Kong Holdings and Hutchison Whampoa Ltd. Li established the foundation in 1980 to strengthen the impact of philanthropy through three strategic objectives: (1) to nurture a culture of giving; (2) to support education reform initiatives that encourage long-term thinking, empowerment, creativity, open-mindedness and constructive engagement; and (3) to help advance medical research and services.The LKSF's grants are concentrated in four areas: education, culture, health care and community. Up to now, its grants have totalled more than $1.45 billion. Li considers the foundation his "third son" and has pledged a third of his assets to it. The Li Ka Shing (Canada) Foundation has been registered as a Canadian charitable organization since 2005 and currently has assets of $897,499,102. Its current operating budget is $28,975,963, and it disbursed $28,311,806 in 2010.

10. Retrieved from www.givingpledge.org

11. *Our Dying Republic: The cause and the cure*; Jr George Dunlap Burns; Xulon Press, 2011, citation on page 182.

12. The news is full of examples showing how the legal framework for private foundations allows financial power to reign supreme. In an article published in the *Huffington Post* in 2006 ("The Gates and Buffett Foundation Shell Game," 22 August 2006, www.huffingtonpost.com/sheldon-drobny/the-gates-and-buffett-fou_b_27780.html), Sheldon Drobny explained, "My background is finance and accounting. I started my career in 1967 with the IRS as a specialist in taxation covering many areas of the tax law including the so-called legal loopholes to charitable giving...The Gates foundation will be in the long run richer than the Catholic Church, which has accumulated wealth and power for over 1,500 years... The Gates Foundation and the Catholic Church have the same goals. They are to keep the legacies for which they were created. For Bill Gates and Warren Buffett it is the control and legacy of family wealth as in the ancient days of the Pharaohs of Egypt. And by not paying any taxes, Gates will be more powerful than the Pope." See also the British Ministry of Defence document Global Strategic Trends — Out to 2040 (www.mod.uk/NR/rdonlyres/38651ACB-D9A9-4494-98AA-1C86433BB673/0/gst4_update9_Feb10.pdf), which signals "the emergence of a global elite, a powerful network of individuals and institutions that sits above the level of individual states and influences the global agenda." The document questions whether it is wise to place so much power in the hands of undemocratic institutions. And in *The Molecular Vision of Life: Caltech, the Rockefeller Foundation, and the Rise of the New Biology* (New York: Oxford University Press, 1993), Lily E. Kay wrote, "Their numerous projects and the unprecedented scope of their financial and institutional resources shaped the development of culture and the production of knowledge in the United States. Through education, public opinion, stimulation of specific research agenda, and the promotion of selective categories of knowledge and research, the Foundation played a key role in the creation of a hegemonic bloc."

13. Joel L. Fleishman, *The Foundation: A Great American Secret: How Private Wealth is Changing the World* (New York: Public Affairs, 2007).

14. Cristina Maldonado, "The Race Gap," *Contribute: The People and Ideas of Giving*, retrieved from www.contributemedia.com/trends_details.php?id=201

15. Ibid.

16. In more technical terms, 3.5 per cent of all of the organization's assets not directly used in charitable activities or administration, if these assets exceed $25,000.

17. Before March 2010, there were additional requirements placed on both public and private charitable foundations, beyond the general minimum of 3.5 per cent. Public foundations also had to spend an amount equal to 80 per cent of the previous year's tax-receipted donations and funds received from other charities. Private foundations had to spend 100 per cent of these amounts. Before March 2004, the general minimum was 4.5 per cent, not 3.5 per cent.

18. Ray D. Madoff, "Dog Eat Your Taxes?" retrieved from www.nytimes.com/2008/07/09/opinion/09madoff.html

19. For a critical account of the ins and outs of philanthrocapitalism, see Michael Edwards, "Philanthrocapitalism: After the Goldrush," *openDemocracy*, 20 March 2008, retrieved from www.opendemocracy.net/article/globalisation/visions_reflections/philanthrocapitalism_after_the_goldrush

20. Jay Greene and Steve Hamm, "Bill Gates's long goodbye," *Business* Week, 16 June 2006, retrieved from www.businessweek.com/technology/content/jun2006/tc20060616_885486.htm

21. Mike Shanahan, "Africa's Water Crisis: A Quarter of a Billion Dollars Down the Drain," 20 March 2009, retrieved from www.iied.org/natural-resources/key-issues/water/africas-water-crisis-a-quarter-a-billion-dollars-down-drain

22. Michael Isikoff, "Edwards used nonprofit to funnel money to Hunter," *Newsweek*, 13 March 2010. www.newsweek.com/blogs/declassified/2010/03/12/edwards-used-nonprofit-to-funnel-money-to-hunter.html

23. According to paragraph 153(1) of the federal Income Tax Act and section 1015 of Quebec's Taxation Act, an organization is required to withhold taxes on salaries, fees, retirement allowances, benefits and some payments made in respect of a variety of programs. In cases of noncompliance, directors of organizations may be held personally liable, along with the organization itself, for full payment of the sum that has not been paid, in addition to applicable penalties and interest. See also Congrès Association de Planfication Financière et Fiscale (2007), "La responsabilité personnelle des administrateurs, actionnaires, fiduciaires, tiers et professionnels: le volet civil."

24. Congrès Association de Planfication Financière et Fiscale (2008), "Concepts juridiques choisis à l'intention des comptables et conseillers financiers." The Ontario Superior Court of Justice's 2001 decision in *Ontario (Public Guardian and Trustee)* v. *AIDS Society for Children (Ontario)* emphasized the fiduciary responsibility of directors of charitable corporations as quasi-trustees. The court held that these fiduciary duties go beyond the mere furtherance of the charitable

objects of the corporation. The case stipulates that although directors of a charity may not technically be trustees of charitable property, they "are, to all intents and purposes, bound by the rules which affect trustees."

25. Retrieved from www.oag-bvg.gc.ca/internet/English/parl_oag_201010_07_e_34290.html#hd5h

26. 2010 Fall Report of the Auditor General of Canada, retrieved from www.oag-bvg.gc.ca/internet/English/parl_oag_201010_07_e_34290.html#hd5a

27. 2010 Fall Report of the Auditor General of Canada, retrieved from www.oag-bvg.gc.ca/internet/English/parl_oag_201010_07_e_34290.html#hd5a

28. In 2007, the most recent year complete statistics are available; retrieved from www.globalphilanthropy.ca/images/uploads/Presentation_to_ICFO_by_Bryan_McLean_Director_Policy,_Planning_and_Legislation_Division_Canada_Revenue_Agency_in_PDF.pdf

29. Retrieved from www.oecd.org/dataoecd/30/20/42232037.pdf

30. Ibid.

31. Ibid.

32. Retrieved from www.thestar.com/News/article/220755

33. Retrieved from www.thestar.com/News/investigations/charities/article/625444--high-flying-charity-grounded

34. Ibid.

35. "Philanthropy on Trial," Council on Foundations *Windows*, retrieved from www.cof.org/events/conferences/2011Annual/trial.cfm

36. Gara LaMarche, president and CEO of The Atlantic Philanthropies, was the prosecutor; Ralph R. Smith, executive vice-president of the Annie E. Casey Foundation and former board chair of the Council on Foundations, was the defence counsel; and retired Pennsylvania Supreme Court Justice Jane Cutler Greenspan acted as the judge.

CHAPTER 6

1. The reflections in this chapter are partly based on "En route vers une fiscalité verte," a study carried out by Agora Fiscalité Inc. (Brigitte Alepin, owner and founder) with the financial participation of a number of organizations including the Ordre des Comptables Agréés du Québec and La Cordée Plein Air. The author's assumption here is that the current environmental situation is disturbing enough to justify the establishment in Canada of an effective, comprehensive ecological tax system.

2. "Australie: le gouvernement va imposer une taxe carbone à 17 euros la tonne," *20minutes.fr*, 10 July 2011, retrieved from www.20minutes.fr/ledirect/756093/australie-gouvernement-va-imposer-taxe-carbone-17-euros-tonne

3. National Round Table on the Environment and the Economy, *Toward a Canadian Agenda for Ecological Fiscal Reform: First Steps* (Ottawa, 2002).

4. Department of Finance Canada, *Budget 2005: Moving Towards a Green Economy* (Ottawa, 23 February 2005), retrieved from www.fin.gc.ca/budget05/pdf/pagree.pdf

5. Philippe Faucher, "L'impasse climatique," *La Presse*, 25 June 2011, retrieved from www.cyberpresse.ca/debats/opinions/la-presse/201106/25/01-4412515-limpasse-climatique.php

6. The data and figures have been taken from the OECD website.

7. Quoted in "Harper's letter dismisses Kyoto as 'socialist scheme,'" CBC News, 30 January 2007, retrieved from www.cbc.ca/news/canada/story/2007/01/30/harper-kyoto.html

8. Maurice Godin, "Visite d'Obama: un nouveau dialogue," Radio-Canada. ca, 20 February 2009, retrieved from www.radio-canada.ca/nouvelles/carnets/2009/02/20/115632.shtml

9. Government of Canada, "Asia Pacific Partnership on Clean Development and Climate," modified 17 February 2009, retrieved from www.climatechange.gc.ca/default.asp?lang=En&xml=4388C861-EF8A-4282-B8C5-FC7D14E29178

10. Peter Zimonjic, "Jim Prentice, 'passionné' de l'environnement," *Canoë Infos*, 22 January 2010, retrieved from www.canoe.com/cgi-bin/imprimer.cgi?id=599762

11. Marielle Court, "Les négociations climat semblent dans l'impasse," *Le Figaro*, 17 June 2011, retrieved from www.lefigaro.fr/sciences/2011/06/17/01008-20110617ARTFIG00590-les-negociations-climat-semblent-dans-l-impasse.php

12. Harold Thibault, "Développement durable: la Chine affiche de nouvelles ambitions vertes," *Le Monde*, 14 March 2011, retrieved from www.lemonde.fr/asie-pacifique/article/2011/03/14/environnement-la-chine-s-engage-a-poursuivre-ses-efforts-dans-son-nouveau-plan-quinquenal_1492980_3216.html

13. U.S. Central Intelligence Agency, "Comparison: GDP (Purchasing Power Parity), *The World Factbook*, retrieved from https://www.cia.gov/library/publications/the-world-factbook/rankorder/2001rank.html?countryName=China&countryCode=ch&regionCode=eas&rank=3#ch

14. "Chinese Economy," *The Economist*, retrieved from www.economist.com/topics/chinese-economy

15. Retrieved from www.chinadaily.com.cn/china/2011-07/19/content_12929940.htm

16. The National Roundtable on the Environment and the Economy (NRTEE) estimates that prices would need to rise from $18 a tonne to as much as $775 a tonne by 2050 to meet the targets proposed by the government of Canada in its 2007 plan on climate change, *Turning the Corner* (20 per cent below 2006 levels by 2020 and 65 per cent below 2006 levels by 2050). See National Roundtable on the Environment and the Economy, *Achieving 2050: A Carbon Pricing Policy for Canada: Technical Report* (Ottawa, 2009), retrieved from nrtee-trnee.ca/wp-content/uploads/2011/08/carbon-pricing-tech-backgrounder-eng.pdf

17. Environment Canada, *National Inventory Report 1990–2007: Greenhouse Gas Sources and Sinks in Canada* (Ottawa, April 2009), retrieved from www.ec.gc.ca/Publications/B77E6264-D0E3-45B5-BE56-5A395C0B7653%5CNationalInventoryReport19902007GreenhouseGasSourcesAndSinksInCanada.pdf

174 BILL GATES, PAY YOUR FAIR SHARE OF TAXES...LIKE WE DO!

18. Emissions vary from one industry to another as a result of a variety of factors and are not necessarily proportional to the industry's economic contribution.

19. Retrieved from www.gac.ca/PopularGeoscience/factsheets/OilSand_f.pdf

20. Environment Canada, *National Inventory Report 1990–2008: Part 1: Greenhouse Gas Sources and Sinks in Canada* (Ottawa, 2010), p. 84, retrieved from www.ec.gc.ca/publications/492D914C-2EAB-47AB-A045-C62B2CDACC29/NationalInventoryReport19902008GreenhouseGasSourcesAndSinksInCanada.pdf

21. Ibid., p. 23.

22. Conference Board of Canada, *Getting the Balance Right: The Oil Sands, Exporting and Sustainability* (Ottawa, January 2010), retrieved from www.conferenceboard.ca/temp/7e45d5a2-b56f-4084-b951-c15c4acf516b/10-169_Oil-Sands.v1.pdf

23. Ibid.

24. Statistics Canada, "Gross Domestic Product at Basic Prices, Primary Industries," modified 30 November 2011, retrieved from www40.statcan.gc.ca/l01/cst01/prim03-eng.htm

25. Retrieved from www.capp.ca/getdoc.aspx?DocId=16169&DT=NTV

26. The Canadian Press, "Pipeline Keystone: Les manifestations s'organisent," *Branchez-vous matin*, 19 August 2011, retrieved from www.branchez-vous.com/info/actualite/2011/08/pipeline_keystone_les_manifestations_s_organisent_7825339.html

27. Quoted in Elsie Ross, "Alberta Oilsands Producers Looking to New Markets off West Coast," *Silicon Investor*, 19 July 2010, retrieved from siliconinvestor.advfn.com/readmsg.aspx?msgid=26696363

28. Retrieved from www.equiterre.org/organisme/sallePresse/communiques2008.php#20081014

29. "Taxe sur le carbone: l'appui des Canadiens baisse," Radio-Canada.ca, 11 May 2009, retrieved from www.radio-canada.ca/nouvelles/environnement/2009/05/11/001-carbonetaxe-canadiens.shtml

30. The Canadian Press, "Sondage: la moitié des Canadiens sont en faveur d'une taxe sur le carbone," *Le Devoir*, 11 May 2009, retrieved from www.ledevoir.com/societe/249845/sondage-la-moitie-des-canadiens-sont-en-faveur-d-une-taxe-sur-lecarbone

31. A number of Conservative candidates were elected in close races while the Green Party increased its share of the vote (Siri Agrell, "Dion Gets No Lift from Raising Glass with Greens," Toronto *Globe and Mail*, 15 October 2008).

32. Manitoba and Saskatchewan elected only one Liberal MP each, and no Liberals were elected in Alberta.

33. The Bloc won fifty of seventy-five Quebec seats.

34. Retrieved from www.statbank.dk

35. Between 1966 and 1988, the ratio of taxes to GDP in Denmark increased by an average of 0.8 per cent a year, from 30 to 50.4 per cent. Even with the reforms, the

ratio has continued to be high, but at least it has remained relatively stable.

36. Many economists believe that the market's regulation instruments are more efficient than traditional government regulation and control mechanisms.

37. Retrieved from www.bioethanolcarburant.com/index.php/bioethanolcarburant/selection-dumois/Plus-d-actualites/Un-tour-d-Europe-de-la-taxe-carbone

38. Arne Hauge Jensen, *Summary of Danish Tax Policy 1986–2002*, Denmark, Ministry of Finance, Working Papers no. 2, 29 June 2001, retrieved from www.fm.dk/sitecore/content/MinistryOfFinance/Home/Publications/2002/Working%20Papers.aspx

39. In 2000, the German government and nuclear industry agreed to a gradual closure of nuclear plants, to be complete by 2021.

40. Philippe de Rougemont, "Allemagne: une réforme fiscale écologique pour respecter eté passer le protocole de Kyoto," *L'État de la planète* Magazine, no. 19 (January–February 2005), in collaboration with the Worldwatch Institute, retrieved from www.delaplanete.org/Allemagne-une-reforme-fiscale.html

41. This idea was suggested by François Therriault in the study "En route vers une fiscalité verte."

42. Categories 43.1 and 43.2.

43. Lenora Ausbon-Odom, "Energy Policy Act: Tax credits await those who plan capital improvements wisely," *Electric Light & Power,* January–February 2007, retrieved from www.ey.com/US/en/Industries/Power---Utilities/Utilities_Library_Energy_Tax_Credits

44. OECD, *STI Review,* Vol. 1999, Issue 2: Special Issue on Sustainable Development (March 2000).

45. In 2010, 80 per cent of Alberta's oil production went to the United States (1.5 million barrels a day out of a total of 1.9 million). Altogether, Canada was meeting 19 per cent of the U.S.'s domestic demand, making Canada its largest oil supplier.

CHAPTER 7

1. Marc Pellerin, "The Evolution of the Government of Canada's Debt Distribution Framework," *Bank of Canada Review,* Spring 2006, retrieved from www.bankofcanada.ca/wp-content/uploads/2010/06/pellerin.pdf

2. Except for the Vatican, the Cook Islands and Niue.

3. Anne Cheyviaille, "Vers un impôt des sociétés harmonisé en Europe," *Le Figaro,* 14 September 2011, retrieved from www.lefigaro.fr/conjoncture/2011/09/13/04016-20110913ARTFIG00690-vers-un-impot-des-societes-harmonise-en-europe.php

4. Eurostat, "Taxation Trends in the European Union: Recession Drove EU27 Overall Tax Revenue down to 38.4% of GDP in 2009: Half of the Member States Hiked the Standard Rate of VAT since 2008," 1 July 2011, retrieved from europa.eu/rapid/pressReleasesAction.do?reference=STAT/11/100&format=HTML&aged=0&language=en&guiLanguage=en

5. Robert Frank, "Millionaires Support Warren Buffett's Tax on the Rich," *Wall Street Journal*, 27 October 2011, retrieved from blogs.wsj.com/wealth/2011/10/27/most-millionaires-support-warren-buffetts-tax-on-the-rich/?mod=e2tw

6. "Bill Gates: 'I'm Generally in Favor of the Rich Paying More in Taxes,'" *ThinkProgress*, 30 October 2011, retrieved from thinkprogress.org/economy/2011/10/30/356718/bill-gates-im-generally-in-favor-of-the-rich-paying-more-in-taxes/

7. Warren E. Buffett, "Stop Coddling the Super-Rich," *New York Times*, 14 August 2011, retrieved from www.nytimes.com/2011/08/15/opinion/stop-coddling-the-super-rich.html?_r=2

8. "Exclusif: L'appel de très riches Français: 'Taxez-nous!'", *Le Nouvel Observateur*, 23 August 2011, retrieved from tempsreel.nouvelobs.com/actualite/economie/20110823.OBS8954/exclusif-l-appel-de-tres-riches-francais-taxez-nous.html

9. Jim Kuhnhenn, "Obama Announces Debt Plan Built on Taxes on Rich," Associated Press, 19 September 2011, retrieved from www.msnbc.msn.com/id/44578820/ns/politics-white_house/t/obama-announces-debt-plan-built-taxes-rich/

10. "Barack Obama veut s'attaquer au déficit budgétaire américain," *Le Monde*, 19 September 2011, retrieved from www.lemonde.fr/ameriques/article/2011/09/19/barack-obama-veut-s-attaquer-au-deficit-budgetaire-americain_1574062_3222.html

11. OECD, "Reforming Corporate Income Tax," *Policy Brief*, July 2008, retrieved from www.oecd.org/dataoecd/30/16/41069272.pdf

12. Loup Besmond de Senneville, "Les eurodéputés veulent taxer les transactions financières," EurActiv.fr, 9 March 2011, retrieved from www.euractiv.fr/eurodeputes-veulent-taxer-transactions-financieres-article

13. Claire Gallen, "Taxe Tobin, taxe bancaire: l'Europe à reculons," *Le Figaro*, 7 September 2010, retrieved from www.lefigaro.fr/conjoncture/2010/09/07/04016-20100907ARTFIG00626-taxe-tobin-taxe-bancaire-l-europe-a-reculons.php

14. "La Commission européenne propose une taxe sur les transactions financières," *Euronews*, 28 September 2011, retrieved from fr.euronews.net/2011/09/28/la-commission-europeenne-propose-une-taxe-sur-les-transactions-financieres/

15. Retrieved from http://news.yahoo.com/ap-interview-gates-urges-g20-aid-poor-nations-134204154.html

16. Mark Blumberg, "Canadian Registered Charities Recently Revoked for Cause by the Charities Directorate of CRA," GlobalPhilanthropy.ca, 12 December 2011, retrieved from globalphilanthropy.ca/index.php/blog/comments/blumbergs_canadian_charity_law_list_-_september_2010

17. "Transcript of Presidential News Conference: Obama Tells Nation: 'This Crisis Didn't Happen Overnight,'" msnbc.com, 24 March 2009, retrieved from msnbc.msn.com/id/29868186

18. 610,000 poor children in 2008; retrieved from http://www.campaign2000.ca/reportCards/national/2010FrenchNationalReportCard.pdf

19. "Obama Unveils FY 2012 Budget; Renews Call to End Bush-Era Tax Cuts for

Higher Income Individuals," *CCH Tax Briefing*, 17 February 2011, retrieved from tax.cchgroup.com/downloads/files/pdfs/legislation/treasury-greenbook.pdf; see also Ryan Messmore, *Obama's Latest Proposal to Reduce Charitable Deductions Would Crowd Out Civil Society*, Heritage Foundation Backgrounder No. 2538, 29 March 2011, retrieved from www.heritage.org/research/reports/2011/03/obamas-latest-proposal-to-reduce-charitable-deductions-would-crowd-out-civil-society

20. Ad van Loon, "Introduction of a BIT TAX?", *IRIS Merlin*, retrieved from merlin.obs.coe.int/iris/1996/9/article6.fr.html

APPENDIX 1

1. Elena Bessa, Contestation sociale et exercice de la citoyenneté: le cas du "mouvement Piquetero" en Argentine, master's thesis, Université de Québec à Montréal, 2003.

APPENDIX 2

1. The gap arising from each of these phenomena is difficult to determine with precision. Hence these figures need to be estimated and the results expressed as a range. This table presents results of this exercise for Canada, based on reliable and available statistics compiled for Canada along with information assembled for other countries that can logically be applied to Canada.

2. In 2008, the Senate Permanent Subcommittee on Investigations concluded that the United States loses an estimated $100 billion in tax revenues each year as a result of offshore tax abuses. (See Chapter 2). This estimate is a product of a bipartisan initiative led by Sen. Carl Levin (D–Michigan) and Sen. Norm Coleman (R–Minnesota). Derived from studies conducted by a variety of tax experts, it applies to an industrialized country that is comparable to Canada. Since 2008, the OECD and the G20 have been doing extraordinary work in trying to stop the losses caused by tax havens. However, as of 2012, the impact of this work has not been sufficient to reduce these losses substantially.

3. According to the most recent OECD statistics (Revenues Statistics, 1965-2008), the proportion of income taxes paid by corporations to support Canada's public finances declined from 12.2 per cent in 2000 to 10.4 per cent in 2008. Since statutory tax rates were further reduced in Canada between 2009 and 2012 (from 19 per cent to 15 per cent at the federal level), it is reasonable to assume that in 2012 the gap arising from corporate detaxation could be as large as 3.5 per cent of tax revenues.

4. Information on which to base an evaluation of how much we are losing from these two elements is limited. It is known that in the United States, the states are estimated to be losing anywhere from $11 billion to $23 billion a year from untaxed Web retail sales, and that tax-free private foundations are worth more than US$560 billion in the United States and C$20 billion in Canada (Janet Novack, "The Last Tax Free Cyber Monday?", *Forbes*, 23 November 2011, retrieved from www.forbes.com/sites/janetnovack/2011/11/23/the-last-tax-free-cyber-monday/; Urban Institute, National Center for Charitable Statistics, "Number of Private Foundations

in the United States, 2010," retrieved from nccsdataweb.urban.org/PubApps/ profileDrillDown.php?state=US&rpt=PF; Urban Institute, National Center for Charitable Statistics, retrieved from nccs.urban.org/index.cfm).

5. According to the most recent OECD statistics, in 2009 tax revenues of the OECD countries represented 33.8 per cent of GDP and governments operated at a negative fiscal balance (-7.9 per cent of GDP). Therefore, the deficit represented 23 per cent of tax revenues in 2009 (OECD, Revenue Statistics, retrieved from stats.oecd.org/ Index.aspx?DataSetCode=REV)

6. According to the *CIA World Factbook*, in 2010 the tax revenues of all countries were estimated at 27.8 per cent of GDP and governments operated at a negative fiscal balance estimated at -5.3 per cent of GDP. Therefore, the deficit represented 19 per cent of tax revenues in 2010 (U.S. Central Intelligence Agency, "World," *The World Factbook*, retrieved from: https://www.cia.gov/library/publications/ the-world-factbook/geos/xx.html).

7. Tax havens: US $100 billion (see note 2) represents between 3.5 per cent and 5.5 per cent of tax revenues received annually in the United States (between US $1.8 and US $2.8 trillion) between 2000 and 2007, the years primarily covered by the various reports reffered in this study. "Multi-Millionaire detaxation": To be conservative, since it is difficult to estimate this figure, we presumed that the loss in tax revenues coming from the "multi-millionaire detaxation" is already included in this percentage.

APPENDIX 3

1. David Stevens, Primer for Directors of Not-for-Profit Corporations (Rights, Duties and Practices), retrieved from www.ic.gc.ca/eic/site/cilp-pdci.nsf/eng/ cl00697.html

2. Canada Revenue Agency, Charities, "Summary Policy CSP-C01," 25 October 2002, retrieved from www.cra-arc.gc.ca/chrts-gvng/chrts/plcy/csp/csp-c01-eng. html. The law does not actually define "charitable activities" and "charitable purposes"; these categories have been determined through common law. Canadian courts have added a further condition that needs to be respected: the interests of the community. See Guaranty Trust Co. of Canada v. Minister of National Revenue, [1967] S.C.R. 133, retrieved from scc.lexum.org/en/1966/1967scr0-133/1967scr0-133.html

3. Canada, Income Tax Act, section 149.1.

4. Ibid., section 188.1, paragraph 3.

5. Ibid., section 149.1. See Canada Revenue Agency, Charities, "Summary Policy CSP-R05," 25 October 2002, retrieved from www.cra-arc.gc.ca/chrts-gvng/chrts/ plcy/csp/csp-r05-eng.html

6. Canada Revenue Agency, Charities, *Policy Statement: What is a Related Business?*, 31 March 2003, retrieved from www.cra-arc.gc.ca/chrts-gvng/chrts/plcy/ cps/cps-019-eng.html

7. Retrieved from www.cra-arc.gc.ca/F/pub/tg/t4033b/t4033b-09f.pdf

APPENDIX 4

1. Université du Québec à Montréal, Chaire de Responsabilité Sociale et de Développement Durable, *Oeconomia Humana*, January 2006, retrieved from www.crsdd.uqam.ca/Pages/docs/pdfBulletinsOH/OeconomiaHumanajan06.pdf

2. *Prélèvements obligatoires et environnement*, retrieved from membres.multimania.fr/cyberbobline/3.html

3. France, Commission des Comptes et de l'Économie de l'Environnement, *La fiscalité liée à l'environnement* (Paris, 2003), p. 13, retrieved from www.statistiques.developpement-durable.gouv.fr/fileadmin/documents/Produits_editoriaux/Publications/References/2003/fiscalite2.pdf

INDEX